MEMOIRS OF A MAGNIFICENTLY MEDIOCRE MAN

My Mountains Are Merely Molehills

Chris Santos

Many of the names mentioned in this book have been changed to protect those individual's privacy. The stories were written to the author's best and most honest recollection, although certain details may have been altered to protect identities and other personal privacy. Should anyone recognize themselves in this book, congratulations to them! They can go buy themselves a medal. The author, however, will neither confirm or deny it. The author doesn't claim perfect accuracy on the events described in this book and is open to the possibility of errors (though they are highly unlikely as the author simply has super good memory). Everything was written with sincere honesty and without intent to smear anyone, but truth is the priority and truth has been known to hurt from time to time. Should anybody offer an alternative take on any of the stories in this book, the author welcomes the disagreement and will agree to disagree.

This book is dedicated to anyone who has ever come up short, continues to come up short, or is just plain short. May this book help you reach new heights, figuratively speaking. It's not going to make you any taller.

CONTENTS

PREFACE

We all love stories. Everyone loves a good story. The only thing better than a good story, is a good true story. Stories of triumph inspire and help lift the spirit. We love to see the hero overcome the odds and emerge victorious. We crave to hear stories of dragons being slayed by the unlikeliest of men and women, to whom we can relate, as we face our own dragons in our daily lives. We cherish the idea that if that guy can do it, so can we. We all need heroes of some sort, whether or not we care to admit it. The hero we choose could be anyone. It could be a famous athlete or it could be a family member (who's not a famous athlete). It could be a teacher who may have had just the right words at a crucial moment in our lives. It could be a completely made up person in our head, in which case it might be in our best interest to seek professional help.

Point is, we want to have someone to look up to, someone we can aspire to be like or someone who can validate us; someone we can identify with and in so doing, feel like their accomplishments are sort of ours. We want to believe that if given the same opportunity and set of circumstances, we can and will shine just like them, because in our minds we and our heroes are so much alike. But are we really? If we're being honest, the reality is that our heroes are way out of our league. It doesn't matter how many boxes of Wheaties you may have consumed as a child. Whoever you may be, I can bet that you turned out nothing "like Mike." As in, not even close. How many NBA championships have you won? How tall are you? Have you had any sneakers named after you? Are there a million kids who want to be just like you? Catch my drift? If you do, then more power to you because I'm still not quite sure what I'm getting at.

Give me a moment. It will come. Ahhh. There it is. We don't hear enough about unremarkable deeds and achievements. Maybe for good reason, but I'd like to think otherwise. I believe there's magic to be found within a mediocre existence, but nobody's really taken the time to entertain even the possibility of it. In this book I'll explore that very possibility through a series of stories that I picked mostly on the merit that I actually remember them. I'm yet to find that magic and perhaps writing about my massively ordinary life will help me. Or maybe it will help you. It is my hope that you at least find some of it amusing, inspiring, even, but that might be asking too much.

You'll soon discover that the bar I set is very low and I'm not talking limbo. Go on. Walk over it. It takes just a tiny little step to clear the hurdle. You don't even need to jump. I mean, you can, if you really wanted to, and I encourage you to. It matters little how low the stick is. Sometimes we all just need to feel the sensation of clearing an obstacle, regardless of its height. You got this. You're gonna crush it. I know you will. Don't expect anything epic or spectacular in the pages that will follow. For every Kobe Bryant in the world, there's about half a billion people whose lives you won't ever read about. Consider this your lucky day as you get to peer into the life of one among those half a billion, mine. It is a "meh" of galactic proportions. If nothing else it should be a breath of fresh air among all the wondrous and glorious real success stories floating around out there. I didn't do it. I can't do it. Maybe you can.

PART 1. ELEMENTARY SCHOOL

The earliest confirmed memory I have goes back to when I was four years old. I know this because I remember my fourth birthday party at our house in the Philippines. I remember two birthday gifts in particular. One was this blue, walking robot with smoke coming out of it. It was cool but I was never really into battery-operated toys. I loved action figures because they let me be the director; I was in control of *everything*, and by "everything" I mean I was in charge of *every punch thrown*. I basically had a one-track mind when it came to playing with action figures, just like most boys at that age. Whenever you had two or more action figures, the only option is to make them *fight*. You try to keep it in context, of course. If they had any type of weapon, you'd have to incorporate it into the scuffle. Still, it inevitably came down to good old fashioned *fisticuffs*.

By the way, I'm a *huge* boxing fan. For most of my life boxing was my favorite sport. No other sport has the drama, personality and storytelling of a great boxing match. I always say that boxing is the perfect analogy for *life*. It's no coincidence that people like to use boxing terminology to describe what they may be going through. *"Down but not out,"* some would say when faced with a setback that they refuse to tap out to. Did I just say *"tap out?"* Oh yeah, that's right. I said *most* of my life boxing was my number one sport. Until around 15 years ago, that is, when MMA took the number one spot. I've been watching MMA since the first UFC event aired in 1993, but it wasn't until I started to learn its intricacies years later that I truly fell in love with the sport.

Growing up I fancied myself a boxer capable of beating up *anyone* my size. I had this false sense of superiority, convinced that I could easily deal with, as Mike Tyson would put it, the *"primitive skills"* that I'm most likely to encounter in the schoolyard. You see, I knew how to throw a *jab*. Or at least I

12

thought I did. During my teens I did get a little more serious with boxing and actually got some formal training for a season. That season didn't last too long but it does sound good in my head to talk about it as though I did some hardcore stuff. At the time I thought boxing was the king of combat sports. I knew about other disciplines, but I had no doubt that whatever other martial arts brought to the table, boxing had all the necessary components to deal with it. Needless to say, I was *so* wrong.

But I'm getting way off track here. Plus, the heading of this bit is "elementary school," so I best stop talking about my teens, for now. Oh, about that other toy from my fourth birthday party, I'm not sure what it was called. I think it was "*Mini-Movie.*" It resembled a hand-held tape dispenser. It played a tiny movie reel, and it had a little peephole you could look in to watch the movie. The one I got came with some Marvel cartoon featuring the Incredible Hulk. It may have had Spider-Man and Dr. Octopus as well. I remember vague images of choppy animations and no sound. It was a neat little device, albeit battery-operated. So you see, I remember my fourth birthday party. That's officially how far my memory goes back. I have other memories that possibly go even further than that, like my *pet bunny running away*. I can still see it hopping across the street as my parents looked on beside me and did nothing. It wasn't a traumatic experience or anything. My point is that it could've taken place even before I was four, but I can't confirm it. At any rate, please enjoy the first section of this book, dedicated to my elementary school years, in no particular order.

1. UNHOLY COMMUNION

I'm a Christian, a *born again* Christian; an *Evangelical*, if you will. And like every Christian who's ever walked the earth, I wasn't always one. Christians come from all sorts of backgrounds and each one has their own conversion story. I'll save mine for later but for now, all you need to know is that I was raised Roman Catholic by two very *hopelessly* Catholic parents. I'm talking about unflinching *anti-Protestant* Catholics who to this day continue to devise schemes, to not only try to get me to step inside their church, but to fully participate in the rituals. The sooner they accept that my conversion wasn't the result of being weak-minded or getting led astray by some eloquent speaker, as they love to tell family members, the sooner they'll come to realize that becoming a Christian is a *one-way trip*. Like a lot of Catholics, their faith is deeply rooted in culture. Though proudly Americans, they hang on to their Filipino heritage like their lives depended on it. A huge part of that heritage is being *Catholic*.

I don't know the exact percentage of Catholics that make up the entire Philippine population, but it's pretty darn big. Essentially, *to be Filipino is to be Catholic*. To embrace any other religion is to betray your heritage and your nation. It's even more personal than that for my parents. In their minds, I betrayed *them*. Truth is, their animosity towards my faith goes far deeper than cultural pride. At its root it's spiritual blindness. There is spiritual warfare going on behind the scenes. After years of countless and ultimately pointless debates with my parents diligently presenting my case through the constant sharing of Bible passages that *disprove* what they believe, I've decided to dust off my sandals and leave it all to God. It truly breaks my heart to have this great chasm between me and my parents, but it is, as they say, *what it is*.

Raised Catholic. That's me. When I was a little kid I served as an altar boy under an Italian priest in Manila. "*Father*

Tortino," everyone called him. He must've been in his seventies or eighties then and *most likely dead* now or he's as old as *Moses*. My money's on *dead*. I still remember his old man face, complete with a long white beard. He loved to say "*Ciao,*" because people got a kick out of it. He was the serious type for the most part although his more playful side would emerge from time to time, usually when around kids. He showed up to one of my birthday parties and performed his favorite magic trick; cutting a small cord in half and magically restoring it by saying his own magic words, "*Peer-leem-peem-peeng!*" I doubt it meant anything in any language, it was just supposed to sound kinda funny. I remember trying to say something to Father Tortino one day using a bunch of English words that didn't go together. It was as though I flipped through the dictionary and randomly picked out words to try to form a sentence. I was shocked to discover how bad my English was.

Still, being an altar boy was fun. I loved ringing the big bell outside to signal the neighborhood that mass was about to begin, and I loved ringing the tiny bell when the priest would lift up the communion bread. (*For the longest time, I was convinced that the ringing was purely magical and had no second thoughts about it!*). Anyway, there was this one particular communion that I will never forget. For those unfamiliar with the Catholic communion, it goes like this: The people form a line in front of the altar; the priest then places the bread into their mouths while an altar boy holds a small dish directly beneath their chins to catch any crumbs that may fall, because Catholics are taught that the bread is *literally* the body of Jesus and it wouldn't do to have the Savior's body lie in crumbs on the floor. After the whole congregation had taken communion, it would be our turn.

On one particular night, Father Tortino refused to give me communion. He gave the other altar boys communion but skipped me. It was a little embarrassing but I was more confused than anything. I asked him after mass why he did that, and he explained that I treated the communion with *disrespect*. You see, I was banging the communion dish playfully against my opposite hand as I walked up front. I didn't do it on purpose. My mind just kinda wandered and I fiddled like any boy of my age. But apparently it didn't go unnoticed. It was supposed to be a holy dish, you know? *For catching Jesus' body parts*.

2. A WORM FOR NED

I've been around a few decades and I've experienced many wonderful things, but nothing will ever compare to the magical time I spent at sixth grade camp. It was the first time I ever stayed someplace else without my parents. I don't remember the exact number of days. Maybe it was three days. Regardless, Camp Foxtail Ranch will always have a special place in my heart. For the first time in my life, I felt like I was on my own, and in the best of ways. As kids, we all want to have a little taste of independence away from authorities. We were not without supervision, of course, as our regular teachers were there and our groups each had high school-aged team leaders to keep watch over us sixth graders and make sure we didn't go full on *Lord of the Flies*.

Camp wasn't supposed to be a regular school event. It was supposed to be fun and laid back, but we still had to follow a schedule to keep things in order. There was a time allotted for various activities, most being little crafts or projects that I can barely recall today. One of those projects involved planting something inside the bottom part of a 2-liter soda bottle. The only thing I remember about it for sure was that I filled it with dirt.

One of my fondest memories about camp, however, was how the popular guys seemed to break character and acted like the rest of us not-so-popular guys. Those who were typically jerks or considered stuck up treated mere mortals like myself with respect. We all hung out like equals. It was as though camp gave them the opportunity to remove the burden of maintaining an image and to be cool with everyone without suffering any damage to their reputations.

As a kid, I never understood why other kids tried so hard to be popular. I mean, you'd have to be a complete dirt bag to be so willing to step on another just to climb the social ranks. I was better than that. I always felt like I was the defender of the losers. It sounds kinda pathetic, but that's who I was. I would seek out the quiet, soft-spoken guys to hang out with and steer clear of the loud, self-centered ones. I stood up for the outcasts. I was their champion. Except, I really wasn't.

Truth is, I hung out with losers because I was a loser. Mind you, I was a different kind of loser. I was well aware of my social status throughout elementary school and even high school, but it didn't get me down. I accepted who I was and how I was viewed by others, but I was able to hold my head high because deep down I knew I was the better person. I was *stronger*. I always believed that if the roles got reversed and the popular guys got to walk a day in my shoes, they wouldn't survive. You see, I had something they didn't: character. Even at a very young age I realized that character mattered more than anything else. It's something that nobody can take away from you. Friends come and go and everyone is one embarrassing incident away from losing popularity, but character stays.

I still haven't gotten to the real reason sixth grade camp was so magical for me. There was this girl, Tamara. She had short blonde hair and eyes as blue as the liquid you squeezed out of those bottles with the curved necks designed to give the proper angle for cleaning the toilet bowl. I was infatuated with her throughout all of sixth grade and beyond. Word was that she moved out of state after sixth grade, but I never stopped thinking of her.

And here's a cool story. I'm eighty percent sure that I saw her again. I was in the eighth grade. It was Las Vegas, of all places. I was watching The Legends show with my parents. It was a musical concert that featured look-alikes of famous singers like Elvis and Michael Jackson. The seats were arranged like in a restaurant, with groups of people sitting around tables. I was certain, eighty percent certain, that Tamara was seated at a table across from mine, and our eyes met a few times during the concert. I took into consideration the changes that her face could've undergone over the past year and a half, of course, and I had little doubt it was her.

My shining moment came during a segment where the performer on stage was asking for some audience participation. First he called out to the women to say or sing something back. And then he called out to the men. At that precise second, Tamara turned her face towards me as if to watch me, and our eyes locked on to each other for what felt like an eternity, as though in slow motion. And that was that. I didn't try to talk to her after the show and it was the last time I ever saw her, if indeed it was her.

So back to sixth grade camp, Tamara was there and it was like a dream. I felt like she was so approachable and that her guard was down. She was there for the taking. It was my best shot. Then along came Ned. I really hate to say it, but Ned was the quintessential loser. He was overweight, talked in a high-pitched voice and was really high strung. People absolutely loved to mess with him because he never failed to give them the reaction they wanted. But me, I was the defender of losers. I never messed with Ned. Until sixth grade camp. I was in the middle of playing basketball with the boys; Tamara was nearby hanging out with some girls. Then suddenly, out of nowhere, Ned came running and zipped right past us. Another kid named Ryan was chasing him. I stopped to take a closer look at what was happening and noticed that Ryan had in his hand, a live worm. Now Ryan was a fairly athletic kid and Ned was not, but for whatever reason, most likely fueled by horror and adrenaline, Ned managed to outrun and outmaneuver Ryan. Ned ran around in circles with no grace or dignity but Ryan could not catch him. As fate would have it, Ned veered towards me and I did what every kid would've done, every kid who I swore I wasn't like and never going to be—without hesitation, I grabbed hold of Ned and stopped him in his tracks. A fraction of a second later, Ryan successfully dropped the worm into Ned's shirt and sent him into a frenzy.

For that one point in time I was one of the guys, the popular guys. We were all laughing amongst ourselves for the teamwork that spontaneously emerged. And it all happened in front of Tamara. Our eyes met then, too. But in her eyes were a look of disappointment and disapproval as she walked away. I was supposed to be the good guy. I was supposed to be different from the rest. Sure, I wasn't as cool or good looking, but I was something better. Until it turned out, I wasn't. I felt absolutely deflated. I blew it. Looking back it probably wasn't as big a deal as I thought it was, and it probably made no difference whatsoever. Tamara was simply way out of my league. It wouldn't have mattered how nice or rude I was, I had no chance. But still, it remains as this one gigantic stain on the most magical time of my life.

3. THE DANCE THAT (COULD'VE) CHANGED IT ALL

It's amazing, that for all the fails I had in sixth grade camp, I consider it among the best times I've ever had in my life. Perhaps it's the world of possibilities that came with it that outweighed the negatives I came away with. It didn't matter what actually happened, what's more important was what could've been. That I came up short was irrelevant. I was that close. Or at least I'd like to remember it that way. I'm talking about my dream girl at the time, Tamara, who seemed within my reach for the first time ever. After all was said and done, it ultimately was the only time ever during all nine months of the sixth grade I might've had a shot at making something happen.

But this story isn't about Tamara, not this time. Believe it or not, there were other girls in camp. But I was too stupid to notice or care. For me, it was all about Tamara. It was her or nothing at all. You can guess what I ended up with. Knowing what I know now and having a Biblical perspective on romance, it was all rather silly. My advice to all the hopeless romantics out there, especially those who profess to know the Lord, is to wait. Wait until you're an actual adult before you even consider falling in love. By "adult" I don't mean being 18, but being a man or woman of God who understands that genuine love, above all else, is an action and a commitment.

While the Lord most certainly uses physical attraction and feelings to steer us towards the right direction, it's not the main dish. For starters, you actually have to *know* the person and not go by the qualities you imagine them to have or wish they had. When you're 11 years old, literally everything you know about your crush is made up by you. It is all in your head. In your teens, it's not much different. It's the age where boyfriend and girlfriend have perfected the art of putting their best foot forward, doing and saying all the right things in order to ensure all the boxes are ticked and the illusion of being "*meant for each other*" remains intact. Also, when two students become a couple, they automatically get elevated to celebrity status, and they become the talk of the town. Sometimes, they even become the envy of the class. They crave the attention and the instant stardom that comes from being an item.

I'm not at all suggesting the feelings and emotions aren't real, for they don't get more real than when you are in your teens. However what's often not real are what those feelings and emotions are based on. It's pure fantasy. You're not really the guy (or girl) she (or he) thinks you are, and vice versa. What you truly are, are two cooperating semi-adults who have a mutual understanding of the social benefits of being involved in a public romance. You know little of what true sacrifice entails. You've not thought about life as a married couple and having to pay bills while barely having enough money to cover it all. You've not considered what it'd be like when your in-laws start putting their noses where they don't belong. That you and your significant other could potentially have "irreconcilable differences" have not even crossed your mind.

Say your relationship does make it through high school. Congratulations. But then you go to separate colleges and get a small taste of real life. You meet new friends. You realize that being in a relationship no longer has the same impact on your social standing since every other college student is in one. You've always known that there's an entire ocean full of fish out there but you discover that it's quite different when you're actually swimming in it. You get hit with a strong dose of reality and suddenly find yourself open to the idea that maybe, just maybe, he or she wasn't *the one* after all. Inevitably, *one* of you decides that it's best for *both* of you to start seeing other people. Breakups are rarely ever mutual. Someone almost always gets *dumped*. It's guaranteed to happen in elementary school and not much less likely to happen in high school. The good news is, if you allow yourself to mature just a few short years more, the probability of finding *the one* increases exponentially. If you truly, sincerely wait on the Lord, you will not go wrong.

So as I was saying, there were other girls in sixth grade camp besides Tamara. On the final night we spent in camp, the teachers put together a dance for the kids. There was a live band playing some contemporary stuff and classics like "*I Saw*

Her Standing There." I was too shy to get on the dance floor. For one thing, I didn't know how to dance. And well, that was basically it. I knew zero moves. I didn't even know how to casually sway my body to the beat even just to blend in. So I sat along the sidelines, not only because of my lack of dance skills, but because I couldn't get my mind off of Tamara.

I didn't mind sulking a bit as it was part of my persona. I thought it made me look more mature. My pity party was cut short by a girl named Hannah. She was blonde, thin and tall, probably had a good 4 inches on me. She was pretty cute, I guess, but she was seen as a nerd long before being a nerd was considered hip. Still, she was a nice girl with a nice face that even her glasses couldn't hide. She sat right next to me and started talking, like she was trying to cheer me up, because I obviously needed it. I don't think I said a single word back to her, not to be a jerk but because I frankly didn't know how to talk to girls. I don't believe I even looked at her. I kept my eyes fixed on the dance floor as she talked away. It took me a long while to figure out her true intentions: she wanted to dance with me. After much beating around the bush, she at last blurted out, "You should go dance," and put her arm around my shoulder. The gentlemanly thing for me to do would've been to take her hand and lead her to the middle of the dance floor. Unfortunately, though I thought myself to be a Don Juan, I was anything but. As soon as her arm made contact with my back, I instinctively leaned forward to reject it.

I never even bothered considering how my actions could've affected her emotionally. It wasn't about her. It was about me, you see. Hannah graciously stood up after that and left. I didn't care where she went. I never even thought of the incident again until many, many years later. Who knows what could've happened had I danced with her that night? I'm not suggesting romance or anything, although looking back that certainly wouldn't have been off the plate. But just going out there and having fun, breaking out of my comfort zone and doing the right thing, I can only speculate how it would've altered the trajectory of my life. It was a dance that could've made all the difference in the world, and I guess it did, after all.

4. THE HEADLESS ACCORDION PLAYER

I love video games. Not only did I grow up playing video games, but video games grew up with me. My first console was an Atari 2600 which I got around the mid-1980s and I've kept up with every major console since. I am a true gamer in every sense of the word. I'm not into it for the social aspects or to be competitive. I'm in it for the adventures, the immersion, and the make-believe. The great thing about video games is that they are within every working man's budget. It is the great equalizer. Bill Gates might be at his multi-million-dollar mansion when he plays Super Mario Brothers, but it's the exact same Super Mario Brothers that Joe Shmoe is playing at his one bedroom apartment. I always tell people that I can't afford *every* video game I want, but I can definitely buy *any* video game I want. Video games are a passion of mine. However, if there's any other hobby that can compare it would be music.

I'm a musician; I play the saxophone. There was a span of about 10 years in my life during which being a sax player is what I identified as. It was my whole being. It is probably the only real talent I've ever had. When I was at my absolute best, I'd say I was a "semi-pro." I've played with a few bands, did weddings and all that. I don't mean to toot my own horn (pun totally intended), but I was pretty good, although accomplished musicians, particularly jazz musicians, probably won't think much of my abilities, and I'm quite okay with that. The Lord blessed me with enough talent to be able to express myself musically and bring joy and entertainment to a few others. For that I will always be thankful.

The saxophone is not my first instrument. A lot of musicians started learning music through piano because it's undoubtedly the most solid base any musician can have. But me, I started off on the accordion, one of the dorkiest instruments to ever exist. Even Steve Urkel played it. I don't know how it came about, but when I was eleven my mom signed me up for an accordion class. I stuck with it for about six months, which is the equivalent of five adult years. It was a long commitment and it paid off. The accordion served to be the key to unlocking the mysteries of music theory for me. It was "instrumental" in teaching myself how to play the piano. By the time I got around to the saxophone I felt like I had a head start musically because I already had a firm grip on the basics of music theory.

During my stint as an accordion player I managed to win a couple of trophies. The big one was from an official competition that was held at some fancy hotel sponsored by whatever national accordion federation thing that existed then. It was a big deal event for accordion aficionados. Students from all over the country (or maybe just California) attended this event to compete. I don't know and frankly don't care how many students I beat, but I brought home the third place trophy. I played the same piece as the other competitors did in front of three judges. At the end of the day these judges deemed my performance the third best. It was no insignificant feat for me to not just win third place, but to actually be able to perform in front of judges. A few months earlier, I couldn't even play in front of family members.

Throughout my instrument-playing days, my parents tried to force me to play for as many events as would allow me. I wish I could say that it was because they were proud of me, which they were, sort of, but they did it mostly for their own glory. In my parents' eyes, my sax skills were and still remain, my only redeeming quality. And boy did they make sure I worked for that redemption. I had nothing else that my parents could brag about. I didn't become a doctor or get some other high-paying job. They knew I wasn't going to be the son who could buy them a mansion and give them airline tickets to see the world. They knew I wasn't going to be the son who'd be able to throw extravagant birthday or anniversary parties for them at some ballroom. No, I was forever going to be a paycheck to paycheck kinda guy. Once they realized that I wasn't going to be their retirement plan, they took it upon themselves to squeeze every last ounce of glory they could out of my music.

It went on for a few years but as I became more

independent, it eventually got to the point where they had absolutely no power to make me play anywhere regardless of how much they kicked and begged and screamed (and they did). The funny thing was, I didn't really hit my musical peak until then. The version of me they got was probably the worst one. By the time I was actually pretty good, I had had enough of their demands and I basically shut the door on them in regards to my music playing. It sure took me long enough, as in, over a decade.

One of the first instances they forced me to play was on the accordion in front of visiting family members. At eleven years of age, I was a long way from overcoming my stage fright but like the next ten years that followed, my parents gave me no choice. I dug deep and convinced myself that I was ready to do it and that I was good enough to play in front of an audience. So I grabbed my accordion, an extra shirt and went out to the living room where the audience waited. I then took a deep breath, wore the shirt over my face like a hood and started playing. Sometimes you just have to do what you have to.

5. TYSON VS. SPINKS

I'm not a very sophisticated person. There are only three topics I consider myself somewhat of an expert on—the Lord (yes, I glory in the fact that I know Him, the Bible says that I can!), video games, and boxing. Talk to me about anything else and you'll get to see my best efforts of looking like I care and pretending to understand what you're talking about. Long before I knew the Lord and even before I really got into video games, however, boxing was my main jam.

Professional boxing is the purest form of fighting. Please know that I'm not saying it is the *best* form of fighting, as that distinction belongs to mixed martial arts. Simply put, boxing does not stand a chance against a discipline that includes punching, kicking, elbows, knees, wrestling, slams, hyperextending limbs and choking. As a sport, however, boxing can be downright more brutal as its rules were designed to limit defensive options and ensure both combatants were constantly in harm's way.

Compared to other professional sports like soccer, football or basketball, boxing is not that popular. The average person can probably name dozens of sports teams but won't be able to name more than ten professional boxers from past and present. One thing is for sure, though: most people know who Mike Tyson is.

One of the most feared knockout artists of all time, Tyson intimidated his opponents into submission long before the first bell rang. He scored an impressive 22 first round knockouts in his career. One of the most devastating punchers to ever step inside the ring, what made Tyson even scarier was his speed, precision, and ability to quickly capitalize on the smallest mistakes his opponents made.

At age 20, Mike Tyson became the youngest champ in history by knocking out Trevor Berbick in two rounds. He was a phenom but was considered by experts to be largely untested.

Many regarded Michael Spinks, another undefeated champion, to be Mike Tyson's stiffest challenge yet, though 10 years his senior and having competed as a light heavyweight for the majority of his career. Tyson vs. Spinks, dubbed, "Once and for All," was the biggest fight in history at the time. It was a match of contrasting styles, with Tyson being the bull and Spinks the matador. In an actual bullfight, the matador usually wins, but this was a boxing match, and the betting odds heavily favored Mike Tyson. He was younger, hit much harder and was significantly faster. Spinks on the other hand, was a little taller, had a longer reach and had the edge in experience. There was definitely intrigue in the matchup, but the smart money was on Tyson.

Mike Tyson was one of the rare boxing personalities that managed to transcend the sport to become a global superstar. Whenever he fought, everyone watched; it didn't matter if they were a boxing fan or not. Even kids were in awe of Mike Tyson because his violent fighting style was nothing like anyone had ever seen. I wasn't like the other kids. You see, I was knowledgeable when it came to the "sweet science," as boxing is commonly called. I knew there was more to boxing than throwing bombs until the other guy fell down. Most of the kids at my school were picking Tyson to knock Spinks out in the first round. During the days leading up to the fight I presented my intelligent arguments for why Spinks would defeat Mike Tyson. Naturally, the other kids thought I was stupid, because Mike Tyson does not lose.

I've always rooted for the underdog because I identified as one. I believe in real life Rocky and Cinderella stories, and Tyson vs. Spinks fit the bill perfectly. It was the modern day equivalent of David and Goliath. Except in this version, David left his slingshot at home and Goliath came with a bazooka. Ninety-one seconds after the first bell rang it was all over. It was the most infamous 91 seconds in history. In fact, I had never even heard of 91 seconds until this fight. One short uppercut to the side of the face was all it took. Spinks went down, tried to get back up and made it to all fours before slumping face first through the ropes. It was what most expected to happen and I was probably the only soul on earth that day who was genuinely shocked by the outcome. That goes to show you how much of an expert I was.

It wasn't the first foolish choice I made, and most certainly wasn't going to be the last. Many, many years later I got myself into a pretty lousy relationship that I wanted to get out of so badly. So what did I do? I asked the girl to marry me. It was my twisted way of putting it in God's hands. She actually said yes. By God's grace she ended up breaking up with me about a month later. I was so happy that I had to fake being upset.

6. COCONUT HEAD

I'm a literal saint today, Biblically speaking. The New Testament refers to followers of Christ as saints; that's all there is to it. It is settled. It's not something a bunch of guys with funny hats determine. I've been redeemed and I belong to the Lord. I am a saint. Now that I've established that, let me be the first to admit that I wasn't always a saint, and I'm not just speaking in theological terms. Ever since I got saved I've been a work in progress, and I'd like to think that today I am more Christ-like than ever. But as a kid, I was far, far from it.

I am an only child, which probably didn't help. The way my parents raised me was all sorts of twisted. I grew up through a storm of conflicting principles and contradicting wisdom. It is purely God's grace that I am such an awesome human today. When I was a little kid, I was awful. I was prideful and acted as though the world revolved around me. Having to recall this period of my life makes me cringe.

When we still lived in the Philippines, my parents hired several maids over the years. We weren't wealthy but we were well off enough to afford having them. It was actually pretty common in the Philippines. Maids were typically female, but at some point we had one who was male. Now that I think about it, I'm not sure anymore if he was an actual maid (or whatever the boy version is called), or the relative of one. His name was Ricardo, and he was only a few years older than me. He was still only a kid. Now I know I said I was awful, but believe me when I say that Ricardo wasn't the most likeable kid either. I remember him to be quite annoying at times. Neither was he too bright. While watching the movie *King Kong*, the one that starred Jeff Bridges and Jessica Lange, my mom had to convince him that it wasn't real. Ricardo argued that if it wasn't real, King Kong wouldn't be bleeding from the gunshots he took from the helicopters. Needless to say, I thought he was a moron.

Naturally, it was my obligation to exploit his IQ deficiencies. I felt so much smarter than him, which I probably was. I don't remember all the details, but I know that generally speaking, I mistreated him. I mistreated and disrespected a bunch of people as I was growing up. Whatever lessons in humility God gave me as an adult, I truly deserved. I didn't like them, but I knew God was right. It's an obvious statement, but God is always right.

There was this one particular incident with Ricardo that was one of the highlights of my unregenerate childhood. He was sitting on the ground for whatever reason, preoccupied with something. I happened to be casually walking by when I saw, just a few feet from him, a half a coconut infested with ants. Now if the title of this entry wasn't enough to tell you what happened next, then I think you and Ricardo would've made a great duo.

Ricardo had a smallish cranium in relation to the rest of his face. To my young eyes the coconut on the ground seemed like a perfect fit. There was no point in speculating; there was only one way to find out *for certain*. So I picked up the coconut swiftly, making sure none of the ants crawled over to my hand, and ever so gently placed it on top of Ricardo's head. It turned out to be about a half size too small, but it managed to rest on his head for a good three seconds before he even realized what had happened. By then, dozens of red ants had angrily swarmed all over his head, face, and around his mouth. Those little suckers moved fast. I don't remember if the ants actually stung him, but he cried almost instantly, like a little girl. It made it all more satisfying to watch.

I confess that it's still kinda comical to me: thinking about what I did, how I made Ricardo suffer, and how I likely made him feel subhuman, but, boy, am I thankful for not being the same person any longer. Growing up and becoming an adult has nothing to do it. With maturity comes restraint and the ability to act appropriately. But this is different. This change is internal. I've been born again. I am a new man in Christ. I'm not proud of a lot of my deeds prior to getting saved, and I feel even worse about plenty of other things I've done after I became a Christian. The difference is, as one of my former pastors put it, I stumble in the darkness; I don't walk in it.

7. SEARCHING FOR A HERO

*G*oing as far back as I can remember, my very first hero was Superman. I'm talking about the Christopher Reeves version, which for me will forever be the one and only Superman. After the Man of Steel, my next hero was Rocky Balboa. I think *Rocky 2* was the very first Rocky movie I ever watched, followed by *Rocky 3*. After *Rocky 3* I then saw the original *Rocky* on video. The thing about Rocky and Superman is, they're not real. A kid needs some hero figure that he could not only look up to, but hope to meet someday. For me that hero was Hulk Hogan.

I guess I forgot to mention that even before I became a boxing fan, I was a huge pro wrestling fan. I thought pro wrestling was real, as most kids in the '80s did. You see, at that time the World Wrestling Federation hadn't come out with the admission that they were merely "sports entertainment," which was a just fancy way of saying they were fake. But me, being the kid who thought himself to be smarter than the other kids, saw through the whole act even prior to Vince McMahon's shocking announcement. The way I saw it, the WWF's larger-than-life personas, ridiculous attires and the bad guy/good guy characters were all gimmicks to get people to watch. However, I reasoned, once the wrestlers got into the ring (and subsequently thrown out of it), the action was one hundred percent legit.

There was always a small voice in the back of my mind that pointed out certain inconsistencies like the wrestlers' seeming lack of ability to block incoming blows to the head, for instance. But a louder, more dominant voice in my head blocked out any rational thought so I could continue to suspend my disbelief. Nobody ever had to sit me down and burst my bubble. By the time I was eleven, I simply came to terms with the obvious fact that pro wrestling was fake. It didn't even take any figuring out. Maybe it was something I had known all along but had chosen to deny because it was so much more fun to think it was real.

So it happened, when I was ten years old, at the height of my willful ignorance to the true nature of pro wrestling, I had an idea which I thought was genius. I would call up Hulk Hogan on the phone and maybe get to meet him afterward. Except of course, I didn't have his number. No worries, unlike most kids my age I was resourceful. So I picked up the phone and dialed 411. I confidently asked Information for Hulk Hogan's phone number and gleefully told the operator that he resided in Venice Beach. The operator paused for a moment, and in his most sympathetic voice told me that Hulk Hogan's number was unlisted.

It was quite the rude awakening for me. I was certain that my plan would work and that no kid had ever come up with such a brilliant idea. My dreams of meeting the greatest American hero who ever lived were crushed in an instant. I did walk away a much wiser man, so that part of it was good. Also, the respect and kindness I got from the operator was something that stuck with me forever. I thought it was pretty classy. It was a great lesson in diplomacy.

8. THE YOUNG
TAKEDOWN ARTIST

*I*n the sport of mixed martial arts (MMA), most fighters are divided into two major categories: strikers and grapplers. Strikers prefer standup fighting which pertains to punches, kicks, and any other type of strike that can be used when both fighters are on their feet. Grapplers like to take the action to the ground where they can employ a variety of chokes, joint-manipulating techniques, or simply rain down blows on their foe.

In modern MMA, all the top fighters are cross-trained in every discipline and are well-versed in both standup striking and all around ground fighting. In the early days of MMA, however, there was little to no cross-training. A fighter was either trained in the art of standup striking, or exclusively in ground fighting. More often than not, the grappling specialists had their way with traditional standup fighters. Once a taekwondo expert or a boxer got brought down to the mat, they instantly became fish out of water and would flail hopelessly while desperately throwing meaningless blows.

As it turns out, I've always had the IQ of a fighter. I don't mean to brag, but I am a natural fighter. I'm not physically gifted, but I am convinced that with formal training, I could've excelled in mixed martial arts. How do I know this? I just do, okay? I have the right strategic brain for this sort of thing. One of the earliest displays of this was when I was around seven years old. I was playing with my cousins and some guests arrived. Among the guests was a boy of about the same age. I had never met him before, and it didn't take long for his parents to boast about him. Apparently, he was a green belt in karate, which from my understanding at the time, was pretty serious, especially for a kid that age. He may have demonstrated a few moves, I really don't remember, but he must've, because he left an impression on my uncles.

The following day, my uncles (who lived with us) kept

talking about this kid as though he was some sort of superhero. Now if you were expecting me to tell you of a grand showdown between myself and this kid, where I bested him and made him cry, well, you'd be disappointed because that did not happen. I've got something better. You see, if I actually got in a fist fight with that kid and won, it could've been chalked up to a lucky punch out of the chaos and sloppiness between two uncoordinated children going at it pell mell. Instead, I made up a story to my uncles about how I neutralized the kid's fancy kung fu moves by repeatedly taking him down. To be more specific, I told them I tripped him over and over by putting my lead leg behind his lead leg and pushing him with my lead hand. It's a rudimentary technique, and there might be a technical term for it, but the fact is, I made it all up in my head.

Yes, I *lied*. But my point is not that I was a good liar, but even without any form of training or ever seeing a real, no-holds-barred fight, I had the right mentality to devise a strategy that would take away my opponent's strengths. It was the classic striker vs. grappler matchup, with the grappler dominating the striker. And this was at least a whole decade before I watched my first UFC fight. The beauty of the scenario I concocted was how plausible it was. It wasn't anything spectacular. Not that my uncles believed me, but in my insecure little mind, the story I came up with was enough to keep my ego safe. It was enough for me that my uncles couldn't prove that I was lying (or didn't care to try) and that I *could've* done what I said I did. Yep, I was Royce Gracie before anyone had even heard of him.

9. THE MAGAZINE

*O*nce seen, never unseen. How true that statement is! And how I wish it wasn't. You probably know where this is going; there is nothing new under the sun. What got King David thousands of years ago is the same thing that gets men today. We all know the story of Bathsheba and how David watched her in secret when she was bathing, how one thing led to another, and how not long after, David was guilty of both adultery and murder. Yikes.

Well, when I was a kid, somewhere between the ages of six and eight, an unfortunate thing happened. My dad brought home a magazine, but it was no ordinary magazine. Something about the magazine caused him to act peculiarly. He was especially sneaky about it when he stuffed it in his closet. Naturally, his suspicious behavior made me curious. What's interesting was that unlike any other secretive thing that might grab a little boy's attention and cause him to pester his father with questions about it, I had a feeling that it was something that I had no business seeing. Rather than blowing my chances of ever finding out what that magazine was, I decided to play it cool and act like I didn't see my dad do anything odd.

Understand that at this stage of my life, I truly had no idea what it was that I was about to discover. I just knew that whatever it was, not only was I not supposed to see it, but it would be wrong for me to. Maybe it was the Holy Spirit warning me. How could I have had the Holy Spirit at that age, many years before I got saved? Well, on this side of eternity, at that point in time, I may not have been born again, but on God's side of eternity, I had been chosen from before the foundations of the world, and I was His, even before I came to know Him. So yes, even before I had any understanding of the Holy Spirit, there He was, whispering to my heart. Throughout my journey to becoming a Christian, there were several incidents where God undoubtedly intervened in some capacity, if only to remind me of His presence and involvement in my life. This was one of them.

So I waited for an opportune moment, and seized it when it came. I snuck into my parents' room, opened the closet and dug around a bit. My dad didn't do a very good job of concealing the magazine. I can't believe my mom didn't find it first. So there it was and I couldn't believe my eyes. On the cover was a lady who had no clothes. At that point I was already committed so I grabbed the magazine, flipped through the pages and saw even more women whose clothes were missing as well.

My sightseeing was cut short when my uncle happened to pass by the door and caught sight of what I was doing. With a stern voice he scolded me and made me vacate the room. Now, I don't know if he was an idiot or just didn't care, but as soon as I stepped out of the room, he went in there and immediately started looking through the magazine.

I actually found the hypocrisy quite humorous, but I was intimidated by him so I didn't bring it up to him until I was a teenager. By then we were both able to have a good laugh about it. Today when I joke about having "an adult reading level as a kid," I'm specifically referring to this incident. Unfortunately it wouldn't be the last time I'd set my eyes on such a magazine, and I'm sure it affected at least some of the choices I've made in life. I can only wonder how it would've been different had I chosen to listen to God's voice and just ignored whatever it was my dad was being so secretive about. I wonder how things would've been had I only recognized it was God's voice.

10. ANOTHER DANCE THAT (COULD'VE) CHANGED IT ALL

*B*y now it should be obvious that my sixth grade year was the highlight of my childhood. Maybe it's because I remember more stuff from that age than at any other time of my early youth. I was on the threshold of leaving my childhood. It was around the period I stopped playing with toys, at least action figures (radio controlled cars became my thing at 13). It was also when I really became a hopeless romantic . I would listen to love songs every night and think about Tamara, the girl of my dreams. When I think of sixth grade, it's all about Tamara. Yes, it's the same one I already talked about. I never even spoke to her. Not a single word.

In my recollection, the single, biggest event in all of sixth grade was THE sixth grade dance. I believe it was actually called that. This happened late in the schoolyear, and it was bittersweet. Summer vacation was near but unlike previous summer vacations, we wouldn't be coming back to the same school in the fall. The sixth grade dance was kinda like the Super Bowl where one can dare to be great. No, it was more like the final round of a *boxing* match, and I was way behind on points. I needed a *knockout* to win. I was beat up and exhausted; if only I could muster up what was left of my strength to throw the one punch that would make everything right. But it wasn't meant to be. Rather than landing the miraculous punch that would've brought about my redemption, erasing all my failures during the previous rounds, I got KO'd.

So this is what happened. I hovered around the edges of the dance floor just watching everyone. I noticed a few small groups of girls going around, walking up to some other boys and screaming, *"No, no, no!"* I wasn't sure what was going on until a group of three girls came up to my face and yelled the exact same words, *"No, no, no!!!"* One of those girls happened to be Tamara, and it dawned on me that she was formally and *publicly* rejecting me. Now to this day I still don't know how Tamara found out I had a crush on her, but I guess word travels fast in the sixth grade. As humiliating as it felt, I kept my cool. I was always good at doing that. I gave the girls a somewhat confused, annoyed look, as though I didn't know what the heck they were talking about. Then they walked away while I did my best to look peeved by their absurd accusation.

But something else happened during the dance. I don't remember if it was before or after this unfortunate misunderstanding, but one of my buddies, Scott, came up to me and said, *"Lucy wants to dance with you!"* A few yards behind him was Lucy, who was looking dead at me with the most sincere puppy eyes I've ever seen. I gave Scott a little frown, turned around and walked away. I did it simply because I did not believe him. I thought he was teasing me or just making stuff up, although there was absolutely no reason for him to. So I basically rejected Lucy, who was a very pretty girl that ended up going to the same high school as me and became one of the most popular cheerleaders in our class.

Now that I think of it, Scott probably walked up to me sometime *after* the whole Tamara thing. My head clearly wasn't screwed on straight for me to turn Lucy down. Had I danced with her, the trajectory of my social life would've been altered forever. Yes, it's superficial and shallow, I know. Popularity wasn't what the Lord had in store for me. One simple dance and I would've been known as the guy who danced with Lucy. It would've been a great starting point for the rest of my life.

PART 2: HIGH SCHOOL

The time I spent in junior high and high school has got to be the best years of my youth. It's not as though the best things that ever happened to me happened in high school. Far from it. I highly doubt that many of you would want to trade places with me during this period of my life unless your life really, really sucked. Even if your life did really suck, it probably only means you went through more interesting things than I ever did.

High school is where you go through the most dramatic changes in your life not just physically, but basically in who you are as a person. Constant change. That's what high school is. It's a continuous journey to find your place in the world. You go through phases. You go through as many transformations as it takes to find that perfect fit. Some of those transformations are genuine and a direct result of whatever circumstances life may have thrown at you. Some are manufactured and calculated to bring about whatever it is you're looking for—popularity most likely.

Teenagers are extremely simple and shallow. It's no secret that popularity is the Holy Grail among high school students. Why shouldn't it be? Once you've obtained it, everything else comes easy. And by *everything else* I mean *one* thing. Nothing is new under the sun. Now I did go through some pretty major changes between the seventh and twelfth grades. I came in as a lost and insecure 12-year-old and came out as a lost and insecure 18-year-old who was pretty darn good at hiding his insecurities.

I did take my lumps and took a few chances along the way, for which I'm thankful. I do regret not taking nearly enough chances. If I could do it all over again I would've been more outgoing, cared less about what others thought of me and boldly laughed at the face of rejection. I also would've tried out for the wrestling team because I would've been fantastic; of

40

this I am sure *today*.

Six years is an eternity when you're that young, but you realize later in life that it was only a vapor. What made high school so great was the idea that the best was yet to come; that my whole life was ahead of me, full of wonder and possibilities. And high school was the rite of passage. I did miss out on having a girlfriend and going to the prom, which is to say that I missed out on everything high school had to offer, at least, from the world's perspective.

Constant change. That's what high school is. As much as I changed during those vapor-esque six years, the biggest, greatest, most significant change that's ever taken place in my life came a few years after high school, when I found the real Jesus, but I'll save that story for later. For now you can sit back, relax, and read on. Hopefully it will bring you renewed appreciation for your life, if for no other reason than it's nothing like mine.

1. THE 3-WAY CALL

*C*all waiting was one of the biggest breakthroughs in the history of telephone. Prior to this feature, if you were talking on the phone and someone was trying to call you, they would hear a series of obnoxious beeps to indicate that your phone line was either being used or was off the hook. When call waiting came around, if you were talking on the phone and somebody tried calling, the responsibility of letting the caller know that you were on the phone was transferred to you. You then had to click over and tell the other person that you were on the phone, because it probably would've been weird to try to mimic the busy signal. It was best to just use human words to let them know you were already using the phone.

But call waiting was just the tip of the iceberg. The body of the iceberg was three-way calling, which allowed up to three people from three different phone lines to talk to each other simultaneously. That's not all. If any of those people had the three-way calling feature on their phone, they too, could make another call to add to the party. Could you imagine the possibilities and benefits of a conference call? Well, I didn't. To me, three-way calling was the greatest feature invented for the pure pleasure of crank calling people with a friend. Whenever a phone call got a little too stale with one of my buddies, rather than hanging up, there was always the option to dial some random number to amuse ourselves.

Crank calling (or is it "prank calling?") was one of the best pastimes any high school kid could have (at least prior to the call return feature, AKA *69). In fact, if you grew up in the 90s, you never truly lived until you scored a few dozen crank calls. One of the things you'll learn about me is that I'm a bit of a prankster. Perhaps for good reason, I don't take myself too seriously. Life is too short. This life is but a vapor and real life happens in eternity, after the rapture, when I've been given the eternal, heavenly body that Christ promised to all His followers.

In the meantime, in this highly temporary body, you had better make room for pranks and jokes. I wish I had a greater resource to pull off some really elaborate pranks, like the ones you sometimes see on TV. There have been a few of them over the past two decades. My absolute favorite is the show called "Impractical Jokers," where a group of friends would tell each other what stupid thing to do to an unsuspecting civilian while being filmed by a hidden camera. The job those guys have is better than any job, in my opinion. There are plenty of jobs that might pay more than what these guys make, but if I could pick any job in the world, it would be to become part of the Impractical Jokers. If you've never watched the show, I strongly urge you to do so. It's really, really funny. These guys are actually the exact same age as I am, and that could be part of the reason I love the show so much. We all grew up in the same era, watched the same shows, played the same video games, listened to the same music.

Of all the pranks I've ever pulled (and can remember), few, if any, were as good as the one I did using the 3-way calling feature. It wasn't anything fancy, but it worked almost as though it was scripted. One day I decided to call a pizza place. When the guy answered I told him to hold on for a sec. I then switched over to the other line and called another pizza place. I told the guy to hold on for a sec. Then I put the two lines together and cleared my throat just to make some noise and let the two guys know that I'm back. They then said "hello" to each other. How I wish I had recorded this phone call!

Basically the two guys were going back and forth saying, "What?" Then they went back and forth saying, "You called me!" "No, YOU called me!" Now if I ever was put in this situation, after a few seconds I would've just apologized for the confusion and hung up. But these guys acted like two of the three stooges. You could almost hear the eye pokes and gut punches. Mind you, these guys were at work, not at home. For all they knew, it could've been a legit customer they were talking to. But that didn't matter. It didn't take long for the two pizza guys to transition into a full cussing exchange. For as dumb as they were, they were pretty articulate in their cursing, almost like poets. That was a good night for me. It remains today as one of the brighter moments of my youth.

2. THE CABLE CAR RIDE

The three-way call prank was brilliant, if I may say so myself. I love making people laugh, but while not too many appreciate my humor, I can always rely on myself to make myself laugh. I'm my own biggest fan. That never stopped me from trying to impress others. At times I succeeded, at times not so much. Sometimes my ideas were just plain stupid and unimaginative. One such idea took place in Disneyland.

I must've been in the eighth grade and I was with two of my best friends at the time. I have to qualify it with "at the time," because no longer are they my best friends today. In fact, I don't really have a best friend today. For the longest time I always saw myself as the best friend anyone could ever have because I was loyal. My loyalty, however, was perceived more as being needy. Maybe I was needy. I was always looking for some male validation. I think most teenage boys do.

As the years went by, as I looked back to my high school years, it became clear to me that I was never the big catch that I saw myself to be in high school. To think that I was, was probably just some sort of defense mechanism to cover up how I really felt about myself. I wasn't the coolest guy; that was never in question. I wasn't cool, period. I always accepted that. But I always thought that I had other attributes to more than make up for that. I believed that I really had something to offer that made me worth keeping as a close friend, but in reality, I didn't. I was annoying, more than a little self-centered, and dressed funny.

I might sound like I'm having a pity party here, but I'm not. Trust me, when I'm having one, I'll let you know. Right now I'm just giving my friendship a fair evaluation from when I was in high school. I did have some good friends who respected me and hung out with me in spite of it all. But mostly, I think they just found me amusing in ways I did not intend to be. Whatever little thing I felt I had going for me, I blew it way out of proportion in my mind. I think there's a word for that. Delusional? Conceited? Whatever.

So my buddies and I went to Disneyland to have some fun, and we had a great time. We goofed around like teenagers and yelled a lot. Seriously, it was like every sentence that came out of our mouths was a yell. It was refreshing, actually. We were all just being ourselves without a care in the world about trying to look cool. Me being me, I took it a little too far. There used to be this cable car ride in Disneyland, called "Skyway," which went across Tomorrowland and through the Matterhorn Mountain. It wasn't too high off the ground. At its highest peak, I'll say maybe it was 35 to 40 feet, if memory serves me right. But it was high enough for me to feel safe from the people walking around below me. Safe from what, you might wonder. Safe from being found out.

I thought it would be cool to squirt ketchup out of the packets I saved from whatever restaurant we ate at prior. So I did. I tore one open and squeezed as my friends looked over the car to see where it would land. I emptied a few packets. I don't remember if I actually hit anyone. I think one may have landed right by someone's feet. They may have even looked up. We laughed all the way. And then we reached the end and it was time to get off. We all had this guilty smile on our faces as we stepped out of the car when the attendant asked, "You guys wouldn't know anything about this, would you?" He was pointing at the ketchup splattered all over the cable car door. I never anticipated that there would be any evidence of my scheme.

To our credit, neither myself nor my friends lost composure. We all just nonchalantly shook our heads, raised our eyebrows and shrugged. The attendant continued with, "Can you explain this?" My friends and I were just in the zone and having the time of our lives. A lowly summer student worker wasn't going to unnerve us. All I said in return was, "Maybe it was the people before us," as we all walked away. We got off really easy. It was a lucky break for sure, as we all could've been kicked out of the theme park at the very least. I wasn't as smooth as I thought I was, but I still didn't learn my lesson.

3. SUSPENDED

I wasn't a bad student in high school. I was the classic "goody two shoes." I didn't get into drugs, I didn't party, and I most definitely didn't get any girl pregnant. Those traits would've been something to brag about except they weren't my choice. I wasn't cool enough for anyone to offer me drugs, so I can't say that I ever "just said no." I don't think I ever got invited to a single party so I can't say that I was responsible enough to know better than to go to high school parties. I was a complete failure when it came to girls so I can't say that I was a gentleman with strong morals.

I'm sure it may have had something to do with how I looked. Besides being zit-ridden from the seventh to the ninth grades, I wore my hair big. I have naturally poofy hair, the type that grows thick rather than long. My hair was a throwback to the '70s and '80s, a cross between Sylvester Stallone's hairdo from Rocky 2 and Ralph Macchio's from Karate Kid. Whatever you want to call it, it was not in style and one of the first things about me other kids poked fun of.

The only thing worse than my hair, was my fashion sense, or rather, lack of it. I went through different combinations of clothing all throughout high school. For the first half I wore almost exclusively Bugle Boy pants. I started coming around in my sophomore year and began to dress a little more stylish. "Stylish" might be too strong a word. *Less awkward* is probably a more accurate description.

In the eighth grade, however, the one thing that defined my style was my *suspenders*. That's right. Good 'ol fashioned suspenders. Like who wears those? I wore suspenders regularly. A typical outfit consisted of a short sleeved button up shirt, tucked in, sleeves twice folded, with Bugle Boy pants held up by suspenders. People teased me on occasion but never in a mean-spirited way. It didn't bother me.

One of my best friends, Ian, however, was a little more evil.

We were frenemies long before it became a thing. It turns out that there was, in fact, this other guy who wore suspenders. Every now and then I would hear Ian chuckling behind me whispering, "*Urkel*," to one of his friends. I don't think he realized that I could hear him, but it made no difference as I was oblivious to the fact that he was making fun of me.

I would later discover that he was referring to the biggest nerd the world had ever known, the very personification of the word. I'm talking about the one and only Steve Urkel from the TV show, "*Family Matters*." Skinny kid with glasses, pants hiked up all the way up to his chest and wore suspenders. And oh, he also played the accordion. Luckily for me, my accordion playing was safely tucked away in my elementary school years and did not follow me into high school. Still, being called "Urkel" by someone who used to be one of my closest friends was a painful backstab. Okay, it wasn't really *painful*, that's over dramatic. But it did *suck*.

Ian and I were pretty tight in the seventh grade and in the early part of the eighth. We somehow saw eye to eye on a lot of things despite the big gap in intelligence between us. Ian was the quintessential book smart genius type, got straight A's and graduated with top honors. Sometime in the 2000s he would start a fast food chain, even made an appearance on national TV, and became a gazillionaire. He's the very definition of success, the perfect example of the American Dream. I on the other hand, am the epitome of *mediocrity*.

"Urkel." At least that guy was a genius. Also, several seasons later, Steve Urkel developed a machine that could temporarily transform him into "*Stefan Urquelle*," an ultra-suave version of himself, and without the suspenders, I might add. Today, I don't wear suspenders, either. My hair is at normal levels of thickness as well. Plus I have little sideburns. Yep, I'm much cooler today than I ever was in high school. It's almost as though I set the bar real low back then so I can clear it today with flying colors. I did clear it, right?

4. PAPERHEAD

*I*an was one of my best friends in the eighth grade. No, he *was* my best friend in the eighth grade, though he probably didn't see me as his. Regardless, we were really good friends for a short season, until we developed a crush for the same girl. Neither one of us ever came close to winning her over, nor did we even really make a move. We did a lot of posturing, but never actually asked her out. So anyway, we were sort of best buds prior to that. Then we had a bit of a falling out not just because of the girl, but due to a combination of petty things.

Starting at around the middle of the schoolyear, we had a little cold war going on. We didn't officially stop being friends. At least I didn't stop being *his* friend. I was the one who kept on pursuing the friendship and trying to make amends. Ian gave me the cold shoulder but from time to time he'd forget that he was supposed to be mad at me and we'd share a laugh or two. And then he'd go back to being distant.

I valued our friendship and still do to this day, even though we haven't seen or spoken to each other in over 20 years. We do happen to be friends on Facebook but our interaction has been minimal at best, as Facebook has pegged him a *public figure*. He's swimming with the biggest fish in the ocean. I think he may have acknowledged me directly once or twice, but that was it.

If there's one thing that really bothers me about being a nobody, it's that I can't be friends with him due to our respective places in society. I live basically paycheck to paycheck while he's financially set for two lifetimes. It just wouldn't work, and I don't fault him for it. If we ever agreed to get together for lunch to catch up on each other's lives, he would basically be doing charity work or else have to come back down to earth and have McDonald's with me. We're literally worlds apart. I highly doubt we'll ever see each other again, but our friendship, brief as it was, will always have a place in my heart.

Towards the end of the eighth grade, things sort of thawed out between us and for a short while it was almost like old times. Like a lot of friendships, we tried to one-up each other in a bunch of things for giggles. That summer we sent each other letters, not to communicate but to embarrass each other. The content of the letters wasn't the point, but the information on the address line. I'm not going to go into detail, but we were acting like 12 year-olds and wrote the most inappropriate phrases that we could get away with on the envelope, all for the kick we'll get out of *imagining* what the mailman would think upon reading it.

When the ninth grade started, we've both moved on from our feud. We were older, wiser and ready to take on the new chapter of our lives, and we each had our separate circle of friends. We were, however, on good terms and still had a great time whenever we found the time to hang out. When it came to pure, raw IQ, Ian was my superior by a long shot. The guy was a genius. I don't know if he was an actual genius, but he was pretty darn intelligent. However, I did have my own brand of smarts. I wouldn't even call it street smarts, just whatever idiotic *useless smarts*.

One day in class and I forget which one, I was sitting next to him. I secretly started tearing up tiny pieces of paper, crumpling it and putting it on his head. His face was turned away from me and his hair was stiff with gel. I could've put a load of bricks on his head and his neck would've broken long before he felt anything was on his head. He was completely oblivious even as others around him began to snicker as they watched the confetti accumulating on his hair. Then it was time for the cherry on top. I put one small strip of paper on top of my head, tapped him on the shoulder and started talking to him. In less than five seconds he burst out laughing and pointed directly at the paper on my head. His laughter was immediately followed by everyone else's as they pointed out the trashcan that was his head, full of crumpled strips of paper. That was a good prank. It couldn't have gone any better. On that day, I was the genius.

5. HEIGHT OF STUPIDITY

At the time of this writing, in my mid-forties, I can honestly say that I'm in the best shape of my life, better than I was in my early twenties. I've still got a few extra pounds today, but I'm in fairly decent shape. I definitely have room for improvement, and I'm still trying, but my cardio is a thousand times better than it was twenty-five years ago, even when I was roughly thirty pounds lighter.

For over a decade now I've been running regularly on the treadmill, and I can only wonder about all the health issues I could have developed by now had I not made the decision to take my cardiovascular health seriously. Fun fact is that I had it planned all along. When I was in my twenties I knew that the day was coming when I would have to put in some real work if I wanted to keep my weight down. I told myself that I would start running on a regular basis sometime after the age of 30.

Sure enough, when I hit 30, my metabolism went on strike. I waited a couple of years or so and got as heavy as I ever have before I finally got around to buying a treadmill. I eventually slimmed back down to my mid to late twenties weight and have since maintained. Sometime after I turned 40, I added pinch of weightlifting to my regimen. Best shape of my life today, and getting better. Just wait and see.

If you're sensing some vanity behind this, you're not wrong. Allow me to give you a little background. I've never had an athletic body. My body type falls closely under the "endomorph" category. I'm not a gym rat or anything, but I've stuck to my workout routines for many years. Most people today would likely describe me as having an average build. The thing of it is, I worked really hard to look *average*. I'd be pretty chubby otherwise. It's actually a blessing in disguise. If I had a naturally athletic body I probably would've never worked on my cardio. I'd be happy just *looking* fit, even if I actually wasn't. As long as I looked good, that's all that would matter. My vanity in this case was beneficial.

During my teens, however, it worked against me. When I was 13, I still had a lot of what some would consider "baby fat." It's not uncommon. I probably would've naturally grown out of it. Just a year later, my body noticeably changed as my shoulders got a little broader and I grew a couple of inches. At 15 I started to put on just a tiny bit of weight, and that's when my foolishness took over.

I decided to go on a diet. I don't remember it being difficult at all. I was just determined to get skinny, and I did. I was legit thin at 16 and 17. I put on some muscle at 18 and filled out a bit, but I was still skinny. I actually took pride in being able to stay at around the same weight from the ages of 15 and 17. It never occurred to me that between those ages, something typically happens to boys; this thing called a "growth spurt."

From the age 15 on, I was so focused on keeping my weight under control that I failed to realize what was happening. I maintained my weight because by going on a diet, I deprived my body of the fuel necessary to launch my growth spurt. My weight stayed the same because I maintained my *height*. I didn't grow. If I did, it wouldn't have been more than an inch between age 15 and 17. I am a very short guy; I'd say a half a foot below the average male height. Just to enjoy being skinny for a few short years, the price I paid was to be short for the *rest of my life*.

I essentially traded my birthright for a bowl of soup. And guess what? Today I'm still not skinny. Just sort of average and having to work hard to stay that way. But forever short. Now it could all be just genetic, my dad is a short dude as well. I was never destined to be tall. But just a couple more inches would've pushed me past the threshold. Oh, I'd still be pretty short, but still, better than what I am now. I'll never know and I've no choice but to live with it.

6. IF YOU'RE UGLY AND YOU KNOW IT

I wasn't always the sexy beast I am today. Okay, maybe I'm still not. But I'm less ugly than when I was a teenager. It's almost as though my face transformed. Maybe I look the same. But I don't. How can that be? A big part of the change in my appearance has to do with my hair. My hair today looks normal. Back in the day it looked like a bird's nest. But it's not only that. For one thing, my pimples are gone. Plus, having facial hair helps balance out my features. Also, the process of aging has enhanced the natural contours of my face, making it look a little more dramatic.

I'm not really a vain guy. I joke about my looks because deep down I know they are lacking, and that's okay. God made ugly people to help us understand what beauty looks like. I spend an awful lot of time in front of the mirror not because I admire myself, but to try to convince myself that I'm not *that* ugly. I have no self-esteem issues today or anything of the sort, maybe when I was in high school I did, but I'm way over it. In high school it's all about physical appearance. The older you get the less important it becomes to you. But when you're young, life could suck if you're ugly. You'd have to make up for it in other ways, like having a big personality, big biceps or a big brain. If you don't have any of those, then you're out of luck. You just hope that nobody notices.

Nobody really ever made fun of me in high school. I mean, a few people did tease me about my hair from time to time, usually in P.E. P.E. is where kids get to lose some of their inhibitions and act like they have the right to unleash their inner jerks. It never got too bad for me. I carried myself in a way that even the sharks knew that I wasn't merely bait, and that should they bother going after me, I'd be more trouble for them than I'm worth. So in that sense I succeeded, narrowly escaping being labeled a total loser.

Now my frenemy Ian, he was the nerdy type but he always

had a good mug on him. As the years went by he reinvented himself and became the complete package in high school; not only was he extremely smart, he was also handsome and athletic. He was never a complete jerk to me but he did grow tired of my friendship and moved on to cooler, more popular friends. Me being pathetic, I tagged along whenever I could, not to try to ride his coattails but just to be his friend. He never straight up told me to leave him alone, he sorta just put up with me.

On occasion he'd be mean-spirited towards me. One such occasion was when I went to his house after school. He had another friend over, Erwin, who was the complete pretty boy type. By that time Ian himself was a pretty boy, and they were two peas in a pod. For most of the afternoon they more or less ignored me, not on purpose, but simply because they were caught up in their own little world. I did my best to hide my feelings, to not make it too obvious that I was well aware of the fact that they didn't want me there. I don't remember what I was doing to keep myself occupied, but it was to appear as though I was being a loner on my own terms, not because I Ian and Erwin were leaving me out.

They finally turned their attention to me, to ask a question. Erwin plainly asked, *"Do you know that you're ugly?"* Ian followed up with, *"Yeah, do you?"* The thing of it was, I don't believe they were intending to be mean or insulting. I think they sincerely wanted some insight on what it's like to be ugly. What better guy to tell them than me, right? *"Do you know that you're ugly?"* How the heck was I supposed to answer that? I honestly don't recall if I actually answered the question. I know I gave them a small frown and was a bit incredulous. They didn't push me. They just sort of chuckled lightly and went back to their own private conversation while I went back to looking busy doing whatever.

What was even more annoying was my own father telling me that I was ugly. I think it happened several months later, or maybe it was a few years later. For most fathers and sons, there comes a time when they would have "the talk." My dad and I never had that talk. Instead, my dad had the nerve to engage me in a serious conversation to tell me that I was ugly, as though it was some big secret that he and my mom had been keeping from me. I didn't say a word back to him either, and gave him the same incredulous look.

Seriously, it's *my* face. Why were they so obsessed? To answer the question, in case you're wondering, it's "yes." Yes, I knew that I was ugly. I've known all along. And if you're curious to know how it's like, it's not all it is cracked up to be. It's much better to be good looking.

7. HOMECOMING DANCE

Another age, another dance. Schools just love putting together dances for students. There's a dance for almost every occasion. The first big dance of every schoolyear is the Homecoming Dance. It's essentially a back-to-school event. Summer's over and the students have had a few weeks to adjust to waking up early in the morning and going to class and all. What better way to raise everyone's spirits than an official school dance? The Homecoming Dance was one of the more fun ones because it had all the fanfare of prom but without all the pressure, like having to go with a partner and renting a tux. It was a *come one, come all* event, and everyone felt *welcome*. It was held at the gym, immediately following the Homecoming football game. It had all the makings of an exciting night.

In my sophomore year, I went to the Homecoming Dance. I looked pretty sharp that night, sporting a brown leather jacket over a fancy button up long sleeved shirt, topped off with designer slacks and dress shoes. I was *dressed to kill*. I even got complimented by dear old Ian during the football game. His exact words were, *"Man, you look cool, I'm gonna hang out with you tonight!"* This was the same Ian who one year prior was asking me if I was aware of my ugliness. But here he was, giving me props for how *good* I looked.

My sophomore year was the year I started coming out of my cocoon, so to speak. I was more sure of myself and my peers sensed it. When I stepped into the gymnasium, there undeniably was magic in the air. The night was young and the sky was the limit. It started out great as I mingled with Ian and his exclusive circle of acquaintances. But unlike previous years, I wasn't trying to tag along. I was my *own man*. I didn't stay with Ian too long. I walked around and socialized with a bunch of different cliques and was having a good time. Then people started going to the dance floor. Not everyone had a dance partner. A bunch of girls danced in small groups. It was different for the guys, though. You either had someone to dance with or you stayed on the sidelines. Can you take a wild guess where I spent most of my time? I stood behind the railing at the foot of the bleachers watching people dance.

After a fantastic start, my evening just fizzled out. I even stopped mingling and just went into full on *pathetic mode*. I didn't even have a plan. You can't go into these dances without any sort of plan. You gotta have a few people in mind you'd like to dance with. I didn't. Later in the dance I was back to being a *complete loser*. I wasn't hanging out with anyone. With the most miserable look on my face, I stood behind the railing, cool leather jacket and all. And all I could do was stare at the many couples dancing. But that wasn't the worst part. As my eyes scanned the dance floor and the walls all around, something caught my eye. At the exit stood a figure with a very familiar face. It was my *dad*. There he was, watching me watch others dance. I felt *violated*. I can only speculate on what was going through his mind, but knowing what a *hater* my dad is, he was probably feeling pretty good about himself as he watched his son *fail*.

Most fathers want their sons to grow up to be better than they ever were. Sadly, I can't say that about my own dad. He is one of the most insecure human beings I've ever known. He couldn't stand the notion that I was just entering the best years of my life while his was decades behind him. I'm sure he found great satisfaction in seeing me, even just for this one instance, not have the same good times he had when he was my age.

8. CALLING MRS. BUSH

*I*f you haven't figured it out by now, let me just tell you that I've always been a bit of a prankster. It's not that I enjoy making people feel stupid, which I admit I sometimes do, but when I prank someone it's because I want to give them a taste of what it's like to be free. I think most people take themselves way too seriously and they enslave themselves because of it. I really believe the world will be a much better place if everybody learned how to laugh at themselves.

One would think that for as much as I get laughed at and ridiculed by others, laughing at myself would be the last thing I'd be interested in. But it's quite the opposite. I love to laugh at myself. It is so liberating. It's like having the power to just step back and look at me from a third person perspective and have a broader view of everything else around me. Maybe because I've accomplished so little in life that I feel this way, but I think that life is generally a joke. I'm talking about the vain things, like everyone's quest for success, fame and fortune. Not that I wouldn't want to have any of those, but most humans waste so much of their lives chasing those things.

For a Christian, the single most important thing in this life is the Gospel. It doesn't matter who you are, how much money you have in the bank or how many European sports cars you have in your garage. It's all for nothing when you one day wake up in eternity surrounded by unquenchable flames. There are souls at stake and God has chosen imperfect people as His primary vessel for spreading the Gospel. I take this responsibility *very* seriously. I will one day stand before Jesus and give account of what I did with the *message* He entrusted me with; that we are *all* sinners worthy of hell, but that He died on the cross to pay for our sins and rose from the dead physically on the third day, and that whoever repents of their sins and puts their trust on His completed work on the cross, will receive salvation as a *free* gift and be assured of eternity in heaven. This I will never take lightly.

But what I *will* take lightly is just about everything else. In the early nineties there weren't nearly as many things a teenager could do to amuse themselves. Old timers older than me would say that's a good thing, but it's not. I'm not the type who would brag about how it was so much better when I was a kid and how we all played outside (Nintendo was already around, by the way, so kids from my generation were never that outdoorsy). My teenage self would've traded everything for a PS4 and an HDTV. If there's one good thing about the primitive technology of those days, it was the absence of caller ID. That meant I could crank call as many people as I wanted and there wasn't a thing they could do about it. On a couple of occasions I called the operator to complain about getting crank called just to see if there really was a way to catch the perpetrator. The operators would tell me the same thing; that there was nothing they could do. With that assurance, I felt empowered to crank call people to my heart's delight.

One night I was talking to my buddy Eric on the phone and we decided to crank call people using the 3-way calling feature. Most of the calls we made were just plain stupid and not clever in the slightest bit. But it didn't matter; we both thought they were funny. Little did my friend know that I was setting *him* up. One of our friends, Darryl, had a younger sister named Barbara. Now Eric wasn't really into girls at that time, but he was very intelligent and would later get a PhD from one of the Ivy Leagues. When it came to girls, however, he just didn't bother. I actually admired that about him. He didn't get caught up with pointless high school crushes. It was true wisdom, if you ask me. I mean how many high school relationships make it past high school? I know there are exceptions, don't get me wrong, but I'd say over 90% of the time high school romance is destined to fail.

Anyways, on one of the random crank calls we made, I told Eric to ask for George Bush. He did, and as expected, he got hung up on. We laughed. Then I told him I would call the same people back, and that this time, he should ask for Barbara, but just Barbara, because it would be funnier. He agreed. I was the one dialing out so I was in full control. Instead of calling the same number, however, I called Darryl. When someone picked up, Eric asked for Barbara. To his shock, the response he got was, "this is Barbara." Then Eric was like, "Hi." By that time I was rolling on the floor and I don't really remember how the rest of the conversation went. It was funny. The funnier thing was how Eric fell for it. That was the whole point.

9. THE PUNCH

Remember about the diet I went on during the prime years for my growth spurt? Well, it worked. From age 16 to 17 I must've weighed barely over a hundred pounds. I was pretty skinny by any standard. It didn't mean, however, that I was a weakling; far from it. It was around the same period that I did a little bit of weight training and a bunch of other exercises. I didn't have any proper guidance and basically just lifted every day, so it was counterproductive. Everybody knows that you're not supposed to work the same muscle groups on consecutive days in order to allow them to rebuild and get stronger. There was no rhyme or reason to my routines but I was still stronger than I would've been had I not taken up weight lifting at all.

One of things I did receive proper instruction for was my *boxing technique*. Boxing was my favorite sport. I loved to watch it, I loved to play it in video games, and I loved to pretend I was a boxer. One of my uncles boxed recreationally. When he came to visit from Canada, he gave me the first real pointers I had ever gotten in punching technique. I learned how to properly throw a jab and a right cross, the two most basic punches in boxing, yet also the most critical. He taught me the other punch types as well like the left hook, the uppercut, and their variations. I had a heavy bag set up in the garage, and he showed me some basic combinations to work on. I only got a day's worth in lessons, but I ate it all up and practiced on my own on a regular basis. My form got pretty good. Sometime later I joined a boxing gym in Pasadena for a short season and received further guidance from a former pro boxer who was impressed with my technique from the get-go. I'd say I did a good job refining my technique on my own.

But all this form and technique would mean nothing unless I actually hit someone with my best punch. Now I had never been in a fist fight at that point, and at the time of this writing, I still have not. Street fights are so pointless. I've always had a level head and never came close to trading blows with anyone, except maybe this one time which I'll tell you about later. For now, I'd like to tell you about this one time when I was hanging out with one of my best friends ever, Chad. He was a big dude. He's only a few inches taller than me but more than twice my weight. I'd say he was easily 220 lbs. and likely closer to 240. Yes, he was heavyset, but he wasn't a total slob. He was athletic for his size. He played football and was a member of the wrestling team. This one night whatever we were talking about led to Chad asking me to hit him in the arm with my best shot. It was an offer I couldn't refuse.

So we agreed on the exact spot I would hit him; just below the deltoid. He turned to his side to give me the best angle, and braced himself. I'm sure he was getting ready to laugh off the strongest punch I could throw, except I didn't actually go for the most powerful blow. I simply threw a left jab. Mind you, it was a proper, *perfect* left jab. I snapped out my left arm, with my hand loose and relaxed. I stepped in with my lead leg in perfect sync with my arm as I was extending it. Right before the point of impact, I turned my hand inward, made a fist at the very last possible moment, about a nanosecond after my lead foot touched the ground, channeling all the energy of the punch through my first two knuckles, effectively transferring the concentrated force onto a one-inch spot on his arm. I killed Chad's arm instantly. The pain was so shocking and overwhelming that he staggered back a little bit, bounced forward, dropped to his knees and fell on his face.

Now I realize he did all this for dramatic effect, but it was also a sincere expression and outlet for the unexpected and agonizing pain he experienced. He couldn't lift his arm for several minutes. I was quite proud of what I did, of course, but when the possibility of giving him permanent nerve damage crossed my mind, I began to feel pretty bad. Thankfully he did recover that same night but he had newfound respect for my punching power. And I developed new confidence in myself.

10. DRIVER'S TRAINING

Sweet Sixteen. I think that only applies to girls. But I was sixteen, and it was pretty sweet to get my driver's license at that age. That was nearly 30 years ago. And yet I remember it, oh, so clearly. Well, not really. But it doesn't seem that long ago. It's interesting how that works. The most common explanation is that the older you get, the quicker time goes by. It certainly seems that way. But as for the past feeling not so distant, I think that's generational. Specifically, I believe it has a lot to do with technology. When I was growing up in the nineties, video cameras or "camcorders," were already common and affordable. More importantly, they were capable of producing images with decent quality. What I shot with the camcorder and played back on the TV was a pretty accurate representation of what my eyes saw in real life. It wasn't HD or anything, but it was pretty HD for the day.

VHS recordings of various stages of my youth are the closest thing to time travel I'm ever going to get. Recently I watched videos of myself from when I was 13, and I was quite impressed with how everything looked exactly as I remembered it. I wasn't watching some grainy film at 24 frames per second and no sound. No, it was as though I was looking through a portal and spying on my world from several decades ago. Everything looks so vivid on VHS. That's what makes the distant past feel like it was only yesterday. I have plenty of VHS tapes that chronicle my teenage years. Some are traditional family stuff like Christmas, New Year's, birthday parties or trips to Las Vegas with my parents. Some are short skits I recorded with a group of friends for school projects. I also have a bunch of pure nonsense videos of just messing around and being stupid with my buddies.

Now you gotta understand that camcorders weren't tiny. They got smaller and smaller throughout the years, and the ones you can buy today fit easily in your palm. The one we owned when I was a teenager was roughly the size of a milk jug. Today most smart phones are capable of capturing high quality videos. If anything unusual or noteworthy happened in public, there'd be a dozen smart phones capturing it on video in an instant. When I was 16 it wasn't like everybody walked around carrying these massive video cameras just waiting for something to happen. I certainly wish I did during this one particular driver's training session I had.

Part of the requirement to get a driver's license was to complete a certain number of hours behind the wheel with a licensed instructor and so I put my hours in. My instructor was a Korean man with a very thick accent. He was serious most of the time although I do remember him laughing at me for whatever reason; I'm guessing I must've done something idiotic. I got to drive one of those cars with two sets of pedals, one for the driver's side and one for the passenger's side, so the instructor can slam on the brakes if needed. However, the most outstanding feature of this car was the sign on its back, which read in giant letters, "STUDENT DRIVER." The idea was to warn other drivers of your inexperience and higher probably of making mistakes, and for them to not only be more cautious around you but to cut you a little bit of slack, especially if you were driving too slow or being indecisive about a lane change.

But we all know that "STUDENT DRIVER" is nothing but an open invitation for others to harass and heckle you. It was only a matter of time before someone would accept that invitation. Sure enough, a car filled with teenagers drove up beside me and started honking. One of the guys stood up on the backseat, turned around, pulled his pants and underwear down and bent over. Satisfied with their work, they zipped past our car. The moments that immediately followed are a bit hazy, but somehow both our cars ended up stopped by the curb. I don't recall if my instructor told me to overtake them, which I doubt he did, or if by luck the other car just caught a red light. Either way, when the cars were stopped, my instructor unbuckled himself, stormed out of the car, ran straight to the other car and started yelling at everyone inside the vehicle. I did not understand a word he said. But it was one of the most hilarious things I've ever witnessed. It was a scene straight out of a movie. He walked back to our car calmly and proceeded with the driving lesson like nothing happened. I really wish the pants I wore that evening had a pocket big enough to fit a camcorder.

11. THE UNLUCKY DECK

I will rarely pass up on comedic opportunities that practically throw themselves at my feet. One such opportunity came to me in the tenth grade. But first, here's a disclaimer. I was not a Christian when I was 16. I may have identified as one, but I was not saved. That wouldn't happen for about another four years. Now that I've gotten that out of the way, we can continue. One day in school, my friend Jared walked up to me with a sly grin. He looked around carefully to make sure nobody was watching and then handed me a playing card. It was no ordinary playing card. On the face side was a picture of a naked girl. We both chuckled. Jared had a full deck of these cards, each one containing a unique naked girl.

The first thing that popped into my head was to ask him to cut the deck and give me half. I hung on to the cards for a good portion of the day as I waited for the perfect opportunity to use it. It occurred to me that in my chemistry class, there were supplementary textbooks placed on each workstation. I planned to slip a card in between the pages of one of those books for someone to discover, ideally in the middle of class. I could only imagine everyone's reaction when the hapless victim inevitably came across the cursed card. I should've left it all in my imagination.

I had the partial deck in my hand as I stood outside of the classroom and waited for the teacher to arrive and unlock the door for us. Her name was Mrs. Herman. She was one of the older teachers, probably in her early 60s, very traditional. She didn't even try to be likeable. She was the drill sergeant type who was constantly looking for a reason. That day, Christmas came early for her. She saw me holding the deck of cards, but just the back of it. She glanced out of the corner of her eye. I saw her. I saw her see *me*. I should've aborted the mission right there and then. But I was blinded by the prospect of a good laugh. Like Hillary, I *persisted*.

I'm a bit of a chess player and I knew that my mission could've already been compromised, so I took some precautions. I made sure that Mrs. Herman saw me stick the deck of cards inside the sleeve of my own textbook, which I happened to be holding in my other hand. This all happened in a matter of a few seconds—me holding the cards in one hand, Mrs. Herman noticing them and pretending like she didn't see, and me stuffing the cards into my textbook in an obvious enough way for Mrs. Herman to take note. And then I *did it*. I managed to stick a playing card in between the pages of one of the supplementary textbooks completely unnoticed.

When I got to my seat I secretly transferred the deck of cards from my book to my backpack. Then I waited. About halfway through there was a *commotion*. It began with a loud gasp then followed shortly by laughter. The card has been found, in all its shameless glory. It was fished out by none other than Lucy, the same Lucy from the sixth grade dance who wanted to dance with me. There she was waving around the picture of a naked lady, confused and amused. Then along came Mrs. Herman to take the card *and* center stage. She was not impressed. Most teachers would've laughed it off. Not her. She *knew* she had me, and she was going to savor the moment. She quieted down the class and gave a little speech to shame the perpetrator indirectly. I don't remember all that she said, but I will never forget the last phrase. She slowly made her way towards me as she talked. When she reached my desk, she stopped, looked me dead in the eye and finished with, "*And he knows he did it!*"

I tried to play it cool but she would have none of it. She grilled me in front everyone. I got reamed. My friend Darryl would tell me afterwards that he genuinely felt sorry for me and thought that I was going to cry. So I sat there, looking like a fool, determined to maintain eye contact with Mrs. Herman as I denied any wrongdoing. The entire time Mrs. Herman was just setting me up for the *coup de grâce*. Her little monologue was just a distraction. She abruptly grabbed my book and violently opened it expecting the deck of cards to spill out. She was going for the theatrics. It would've been checkmate. But there was *nothing*. I saw her expression change from that of domination to total bewilderment. She was flabbergasted. I ruined her Christmas. She desperately flipped through the pages hoping to find something but not a single playing card was in the book. Why she didn't move on to search my backpack I couldn't tell you. Perhaps at that moment she came to the realization that I was a step ahead of her and that any further attempts to find the smoking gun would only make her look foolish. But make no mistake about it; I *lost* this one, big time. I was more than lucky that she didn't find the cards. It wouldn't have been the end of the world but it would've made my humiliation complete. As it stood, it was *inconclusive*.

That wasn't the end of it, though. Later that day I was called in to the vice principal's office. He was a jolly kind of guy. He used to be a teacher at my elementary but I don't think he remembered me. It was a lot more pleasant sitting in front of him one on one than getting interrogated by Mrs. Herman in front of the whole class. I told him that while I did have in my possession some playing cards with naked women on it, I wasn't the only one who had any. I swore that I wasn't the culprit and that anybody could've done it. He then asked, "If so many other students have these cards, then why were you the only one to get caught?" I calmly and plainly responded, "*Bad luck*." Then *that* was the end of it. Remember, disclaimer, I wasn't a Christian.

12. FIRST DATE

I had my first date when I was sixteen. I think that's a fairly standard age for most to have experienced their very first date. However, I am a little reluctant to call it an actual date for a few reasons. First off, there were three of us. My friend Chad, you know, that big dude I knocked down with one punch? He tagged along. Second, it wasn't like my date and I were all over each other. Not even close. We behaved like friends towards each other for the most part, although admittedly somewhat flirtatious. Still, it wasn't like we were holding hands or anything of the sort. Lastly, nothing ever became of it. We just remained friends and she never ever told me that she had feelings for me.

My date was Marissa. She was my sophomore year crush. We went to the same elementary school but never spoke to each other until high school. I took her (and Chad) to Medieval Times in Buena Park on a Friday night. It was fun, even took a picture with just me and her. Afterwards we walked around Beach Blvd., past Knott's Berry Farm and whatever else was around there. Chad hung back and gave Marissa and me some space. We walked side by side and I remember playfully bumping her with my shoulder repeatedly because you know, that was like the smooth thing to do, right? At some point we spontaneously started spinning around together, and if that wasn't romantic then I don't know what is. Okay fine, it wasn't *that* romantic, but maybe, just maybe, Marissa was enjoying my company that evening. She looked like she was having a good time. It actually wasn't the first time she ever went anywhere with me. Just a few months earlier, I took her to a family Christmas party, and technically, that was more of a date than this one, except for the fact that she had a boyfriend. To be honest, I don't remember how I pulled that one off or how I managed not to get beat up by her boyfriend after. But when I took Marissa (and Chad) to Medieval Times, she was as single as a dollar bill. That night was magical at least for me. Although in retrospect I hesitate to fully commit to calling it a date, on that evening, nearly 30 years ago, it sure felt like one to me.

The way I asked her to go with me was equally exciting. I was a bit of a schemer, you see. I instructed Chad to call Marissa on the phone, talk to her for a short while and then call me on 3-way but on the pretense that I had no idea Marissa was listening in on the other line. So Chad did as I asked, called Marissa, chatted with her and then proceeded to call me on 3-way. After a little while the topic of Marissa finally came up, and I started telling Chad how in love I was with Marissa; it was part of my plan. It wasn't really news to Marissa because it was obvious that I had a major crush on her. It was more of an open secret. That Marissa didn't flat out reject me prior was enough encouragement for me to keep pursuing her. I finally got around to mentioning to Chad how I wanted to take Marissa to Medieval Times, but that I was afraid she'd turn me down. That was Chad's cue to "surprise" me by saying, *"Hey Marissa, would you go to Medieval Times with him?"* I acted a little confused and said something along the lines of, *"Huh? What are you talking about?"* Chad asked her once more and I was like, *"Yeah right, whatever, very funny, man!"* Marissa burst out laughing before she was able to say an actual word. Naturally, I did my best to act surprised and embarrassed, and did a pretty good job. After she had gathered herself, she simply said, *"Yes!"* And I responded with, *"What?"* And again she said, *"Yes!"* Then I asked, *"For real? You'd go to Medieval Times with me?"* And for the third time she said, *"Yes!"* It was a perfectly executed plan. And the rest is history.

13. THE GREATEST SNUB

I haven't met a lot of famous people. Almost all of the famous people I've met are professional boxers. By "meet" I mean shaking their hand or taking a picture with them. Pro boxers are the most accessible professional athletes you'll ever find, in large part because it's an individual sport and as an individual, these guys have a lot more freedom. They're not part of a team or an organization. Most of them also don't have the same kind of endorsements sports teams do, and they don't have to consult with their agents every single time they go out in public.

My favorite boxer of all time is Manny Pacquiao. I first saw him fight on the undercard of Lennox Lewis vs. Mike Tyson back in 2002. I became an instant fan of his exciting style. One thing I have in common with Pacquiao besides our heritage is that he was raised Catholic but later became a Christian. Prior to Pacquiao's conversion, I actually prayed for him on occasion that he might come to a saving knowledge of Jesus Christ.

But before there was Manny Pacquiao, my favorite boxer was Evander Holyfield. You may know him as the guy whose ear got bitten off by Mike Tyson. That happened in their rematch. The first time they fought, Holyfield knocked him out. Holyfield, considered to be past his prime after many brutal wars in the ring, was a huge underdog in their first fight. He proved just about everybody wrong when he stopped Tyson in the tenth round. Evander Holyfield was instrumental to my journey to salvation. The way he spoke about Jesus— that personal relationship that he had—was something I envied, and the Lord used that to lead me to the truth.

But before Holyfield, Muhammad Ali was my absolute favorite boxer of all time, though he retired long before I ever became a boxing fan. I watched as many fights of his on video as I could get my hands on. He was basically a superhero to me. As a little kid I wanted to meet Hulk Hogan but never did.

I wasn't going to let that happen with Muhammad Ali. When I was 17, I got the opportunity to meet Ali at an official autograph signing at some hotel. I brought with me a picture book about Ali for him to sign. In line there was this goofy dad who was gawking at Muhammad Ali. The guy had curly blonde hair and had his kid, who was probably no more than 3 years old, sitting on his shoulders. The guy just went on and on about how much he loved Ali. The closer we got to Ali the more unreal it felt. I couldn't believe I stood only a few feet away from him. There he was sitting on a chair signing autographs and joking with people. At that stage of Ali's life, his speech was pretty slurred. Beside him was an interpreter whose job was to clarify what Ali was trying to say. At one point I heard Ali say something to one of the fans. His interpreter then told the fan, *"He said you're not as dumb as you look,"* which caused everybody around to laugh. When it was the goofy guy's turn to get an autograph, Ali took his kid, started making faces at him (or her, I don't recall) and gave him a kiss before handing him back to his goofy dad. *My* dad was there and got the whole thing on video. Mr. Goofy Guy afterwards hounded my dad and got his number so that he could get a copy of the footage of Muhammad Ali holding his kid.

And then came my turn, finally. I stood beside Ali and I don't remember if I said anything to him. I handed him the picture book and he proceeded to sign his name on the front cover. My dad took a picture. The only thing wrong with the picture was that Ali was looking down, signing the book. But that would've been fine had it not been for the fact that Ali basically ignored me. Not once did he make eye contact with me. He didn't utter a word, didn't try to playfully insult me or anything. I don't necessarily blame him considering his physical condition and how tired he must've been not just that day, but for having to do these autograph sessions several times a year in different parts of the country. It didn't help that I was naturally shy and made no attempts to egg him on the way other people in line did (some guy kept yelling at Ali, *"You're still pretty, champ!"*). I didn't give Ali anything to work with or any reason to say something to me. So he just took the book, wrote his name on it and gave it back to me. Actually it may have been his interpreter who passed the book to me. I can't even say that Ali handed me back the book he signed. No, he gave it to his interpreter, who in turn gave it to me.

It was an awesome occasion to have met one of my heroes, but at the same time so disappointing that he didn't even acknowledge my presence. It almost reminds me of the scene from the classic movie, *A Christmas Story*, when Ralphie finally got to meet Santa Clause, only for his hopes and dreams to get crushed by the very man he hoped would make them come true. At least Ralphie was able to salvage the situation. I did make up for it around a quarter of a century later, when I would meet Dustin Poirier, the then UFC lightweight champion. It was at another autograph signing. I wasn't his biggest fan, but I was a fan *enough*. He's nowhere near Ali's status and hardly anyone besides the most hardcore UFC fan has heard of him, but it was a much better experience than Ali. I was able to take a good picture with him and even had a brief conversation. I wish him all the luck in the world.

14. THE SECRET WEAPON

I took great pride in my boxing skills when I was in high school. I had great punching form, could throw nice combinations on the heavy bag, and could even work the speed bag a bit. The truth is, while I spent plenty of hours working on combinations and dancing around the heavy bag in the garage, I didn't have any experience in actual sparring. Everything in my head was all theory. I was no different from a child who was convinced he's a ninja after earning his yellow belt in Taekwondo. Still, it made me feel like I wasn't at the bottom of the food chain and that I could take care of myself if push came to shove.

To me, fighting never made any sense outside the context of a professional, organized event for which both combatants got handsomely compensated. Street fights are stupid. You'd have to be the lowest of lowlifes to believe that winning a street fight has any meaning. It doesn't necessarily mean you're the better man. It just means you're the better fighter. You could still totally suck at school, at your job, or at relationships. You could suck at singing or dancing. You could still suck at life much worse than the guy you just incapacitated. I guess there's some consolation in that. *Yes, my life sucks but I'm not the one laying in a pool of my own blood!* It's so petty. Depending on what stage of your life you get into a fist fight, consequences may vary. At elementary school level you might end up with a black eye or a bloody nose. In high school and beyond, the injuries could be more severe and you could end up in a hospital or worse.

Outside of the physical consequences, you also have to worry about getting punished. Again, it's pretty easy if you're a kid. You might be handed a detention slip or you can get suspended. Your parents might ground you or not give you any allowance. But if you're an adult, you can be thrown in jail and end up owing someone a ton of money. This is why I don't fight. It's just the dumbest, most pointless thing you can participate in. If you give in to your anger and just let your fists fly then you're liable to throw all strategy out the window and start flailing like an ape. However, if your head is cool enough to be able to fight intelligently in a calm, calculated manner, then you're also cool enough to let reason prevail and just walk away from the situation.

Fights are void of sound logic. This is why the one time I almost got into one was one of the dumbest memories of my life. For one thing, it would've been against one of the best friends I've ever had, Darryl. Yup, the same one who has a sister named Barbara. I don't even remember what we would've fought each other for. We had some disagreement about something, I'm guessing, leading to words that never should've come out of our mouths. If we started swinging at each other right there and then, it would've made more sense. But Darryl, like me, was also pretty level-headed. It takes two to tango, as they say, and neither of us wanted to dance. Disclaimer—I still wasn't a Christian at this point, and I walked in the flesh. My flesh told me that I couldn't let my pride down by simply walking away from whatever it was that was so insignificant I don't remember a thing about it today. So I threw down the gauntlet and challenged Darryl to a fight after school. He agreed, and we set up the time and place. We gave it time to build up and marinate so that when the moment came, we'd be psyched up for the big showdown.

Now I seriously didn't know what I was thinking when I did this and I had no idea how it was going to unfold. I guess deep down I was hoping that it would just fizzle out. I liked to play mind games, even if I wasn't as good at it as I thought I was. So just to sound more confident, I warned Darryl that I had a "*secret weapon*." I don't think he cared, and I can't tell you how he felt about this whole thing as we never talked about it after. I don't even remember any of the details, but when Darryl and I arrived at the place we agreed on, we both had the same look on our faces; *this was lame*. Without so much as saying a word, we just acknowledged what a dumb idea it was. I don't think either of us was actually expecting us to fight each other, especially Darryl. He probably thought I was full of it; and I was. I knew he had it in him to get into a fight, but he knew I wasn't that type of guy. We were really good friends, and a big part of our friendship was based on being level-headed and having the ability to step back and just shake our heads at all the nonsense, which is what we did that afternoon. And as a parting gift, I revealed to him what my secret weapon was; a *mouth guard*. You know, those rubbery things that boxers put inside their mouths to protect their teeth. That was my secret weapon. The idea behind it was that with my pearly whites protected, I could fight more aggressively and therefore be more dangerous since I wouldn't have to worry about getting a tooth punched out. And for the record, if Darryl and I had actually ended up fighting each other, I would've lost. He would probably have had enough restraint to not hurt me seriously, but I would've been embarrassed.

15. THE OTHER SECRET WEAPON

*B*y now you should know that boxing is one of my favorite sports (today MMA is #1 in my book). I simply love the simplicity of it. To me it represents life. A lot of the things that happen inside the boxing ring could be used as an analogy for life; down but not out, giving it your best shot, taking it on the chin, etc. Despite the violent nature of boxing, I have zero convictions as a Christian, about loving it. To me it's never been about rooting for one guy to get seriously hurt or injured, but for one guy to overcome the odds and show his determination. One of the things I used to always say about boxing is that the sport was designed to glorify the human body. The rules are fashioned in a way to give humans the opportunity to prove their strength, toughness, and endurance.

For those who are physically gifted enough to box professionally, it is a lifelong opportunity to continually push their bodies to the limits and overcome every obstacle. To me it ultimately brings glory to God. I truly wish I had the natural athleticism and toughness to have become a fighter. I believe that tough guys know that they are tough. If you listen to your body, you'll find that it's pretty honest in communicating to your mind how far you should push it to do anything. My body tells me that I am not tough *at all*. I can sense how frail I am. I know that if I took one good shot on the chin from anyone around my size, my lights will go out. I don't believe that my head's architecture is optimized for absorbing big impacts. Some people's heads have the natural contours and the supporting musculature to be able to take strong punches, but I don't. I came to accept long ago that the extent of my participation in boxing is being a spectator and playing it in a video game.

One sport that I have very little interest in is football. I'm talking about *American football*, just to be clear. I was never into the NFL because when I was growing up, my dad was only interested in basketball and boxing. I know there's a lot of complexity involved in any single play in football, but to me, football is a sport where the action lasts for 10 seconds at a time, followed by inaction that lasts a couple of minutes. That never appealed to me. But while watching football could be boring, *playing* it is a whole other thing.

Now I'm nowhere big enough to have played football in high school, but I did play with a bunch of other guys my size this one time after school. It was just for fun, none of us had gear or even proper footwear, but it was on the actual football field. I happened to be walking by and they needed an extra player to make things even. They asked if I wanted to join, so I did. When the other team kicked off, I ended up catching the football. It wasn't even a clean catch and I almost dropped the ball. The rest of my team started screaming at me to run, and I started running towards the goal. It turned out to be the run of my life. I've always had great footwork and reflexes, which made up for my lack of natural athleticism. I saw a guy running full speed trying to intersect me. I stopped on a dime at the precise moment and watched the guy fall to the ground. I continued my run and saw multiple guys coming after me. I faked one direction, stopped and switched directions, sending a couple of guys falling to the ground. I did this at least a couple more times, successfully evading my pursuers until finally, one guy, who had this very determined look on his face, started sprinting towards me. He wasn't going to fall for my jukes, and I tried, but he was able to finally bring me down by diving for my legs. The entire sequence was gloriously epic. I was quite proud of myself especially considering the fact that I've never really played football. I don't think I did anything else remarkable for the rest of the game, but I had that one moment. A few of the guys from the other team started shouting *"secret weapon"* at me, and it felt good.

16. ACADEMIC DECATHLON

I'm really not that stupid. I'm stupid in a lot of ways, but I wasn't a dumb guy in high school. My grades were comfortably above average. I was an underachiever growing up. It's not something I'm proud of. I'm smart in a lot of ways, too, but I never put too much effort behind my God-given intelligence. To say that it all went to waste would be an exaggeration, but more than that, admitting that even a small percentage of it went to waste is more than a little painful. I wasn't the most ambitious kid. I was naturally lazy. This laziness was reinforced by my parents. Now I really hate to do this because I'm not one of those people who blame their childhood for everything that's wrong with their adulthood, but in this case, I'm sad to say that my parents did play a vital role in my overall lack of drive to push myself beyond my known limits when it came to a lot of things, school included.

My parents are extremely prideful. The most important thing to them was what their friends and relatives thought about them. A lot of the decisions they made was motivated by how they felt it would affect their image. They wanted to have prestige in their circles. They did everything they could to maintain the appearance of success, and it ultimately cost them. One of their favorite ways to toot their own horn was to always tell me that my future was set because of *them*; that they'll give me a house when I become an adult and enough money to give me a head start in life. When you're a little kid, you sort of just believe all of this even if you don't have a concept of what being a responsible adult even entails. You hear this kind of fairytale often enough from anyone, let alone your own parents, and it'll go to your head. I let it get to mine and when things got a little challenging in college, I didn't have the motivation to push myself. By then I had stopped buying into my parents' empty promises, especially in light of how badly in debt they were and the several foreclosures they'd gone through.

Still, being self-driven doesn't happen overnight. It takes years of practice and encouragement from a trusted source. It's a seed that needs to be planted very early on and must be regularly watered. I never had that seed. All I had was my parents telling me that I'm *set for life*. In the back of my mind I was thinking, *why even bother?* When I needed it the most, I didn't have the power to flip the switch and instantly become motivated, even if I knew for a fact that my future depended on it. Disclaimer: I was not a Christian yet. I didn't have the guidance of the Holy Spirit and was missing the wisdom to do the right thing. I know that it doesn't take being a Christian to achieve financial success. In fact, most people who are rich are not Christians. Jesus said so Himself, that it'd be easier for a camel to go through the eye of the needle than for a rich man to enter heaven. I'm not using my lack of salvation as an excuse, but I most definitely would've benefited from having access to God's infinite wisdom then. Instead, I was a slave to the flesh and my natural tendencies to underachieve and be lazy, not having the supernatural means to overcome it. I never finished college and have spent the last 15 years regretting it.

In high school, though, I had flashes of brilliance. From time to time I would seem pretty bright. I had good enough grades to become part of the Academic Decathlon Team when I was a senior. The team consisted of around a dozen juniors and seniors. The Academic Decathlon was basically a day-long Olympic-like event where schools from all over the state competed against each other in various academic categories. One was essay writing. I don't remember what I wrote about, but I do remember quoting, *"Man does not live by bread alone,"* and tying it to whatever the topic was. I knew that I did a good job. It didn't matter how well I placed, I could be proud of my work. My only regret is not having obtained a copy of it so I can see whatever the heck it was that I wrote. The winners from each category would be revealed that same day in the evening in the gymnasium, after dinner was served.

When the Master of Ceremonies finally got to announcing the winners of the essay writing, I had a good feeling that I would place, until she announced the third place winner. I was instantly deflated when she mentioned someone else's name. I knew that I couldn't possibly get top honors on this and that if

I got any, it would've been third place. So that was it for me after thinking I did really well. Then the MC would go on to announce the second and first place winners. The gold medalist's name sounded a lot like mine, both first and last names. Plus, his high school had the same name as my high school. And then it hit me. I had won. I got *first place* in essay. I took home the *only* gold medal for my high school. I even bested my friend, Ian, that super smart one who is now a trillionaire. He was part of the Academic Decathlon team as well and was our school's favorite to bring home any medal. I couldn't believe it ended up being me.

17. PICK UP (CON) ARTIST

Chad is one of the best friends I've ever had in high school. We remained good friends throughout high school and a little while after, but as a lot of friendships go, we eventually went our separate ways. We still keep in touch through Facebook, and talk on the phone occasionally, as in once every couple of years or so, if even that much. We've known each other for *30 years*. I remember one particular summer in the eighth grade. He stayed a couple of days at my house. We had a blast just being teenagers, talking about life, playing video games and contemplating our futures.

At age 14, you think you're close to being a man and yet not that far removed from being a kid. During those two days, however, we were *kids*. We had a great time and my parents were frankly sick of his company. They like him, but as my dad liked to say then, *"first day a guest, second day a burden, third day a pest,"* only they skipped a day and promoted Chad from guest to pest in just two days. On the night of his second day we drove him home. Chad was scheduled to fly to Kansas City in a few days to stay there for most of the summer. It was the last time we would see each other until school started again in the fall. During the drive we were both pretty bummed out about it. We had a conversation in the backseat that we would forever refer to as *"30 more hours."* We both wished that we had an extra 30 hours to hang out. As fate would have it, when we arrived at his house, nobody was home. We waited several minutes to see if anyone would answer the door but no one ever did. We could've just left him there, but my parents wouldn't have it, so they decided to take Chad back home with us for the night, as annoyed as they were. Just like that, our wish for 30 more hours was granted.

Chad and I were confidants, especially when it came to matters of the opposite sex. That's a big deal in high school. You needed to have someone you can talk to about your crushes, who you thought was cute, and who you wanted to ask out. You needed male validation and someone who would tell you to "*go for it*." And when you ultimately get rejected by the girl, you needed someone to tell you that "*she wasn't worth it*" or that "*it was her loss*." That's who Chad was to me, and that's who I was to him. There was this Filipina girl (okay, that's redundant, I know) in our geometry class in the tenth grade that Chad was mildly interested in. Chad had zero problems talking to girls or anybody. He's the perfect salesman type who can talk forever and B.S. his way through any conversation. Shy he was not. He's got an outgoing personality and makes a great first impression on total strangers at parties. Basically the opposite of me. He didn't need any help from a guy like me, especially when it came to talking to girls.

But I happened to be Filipino and he wanted to charm the girl by saying something to her in *Tagalog* (that's the main Filipino language, in case you were wondering). So I taught him this phrase to say to her, which I guaranteed Chad would win him brownie points. "*Mamahalin mo ba ako kahit payat ako?*" I wrote it down for him so he can practice it. He asked me what it meant, but I told him to just trust me. He was a little bit hesitant, but I reassured him that he would not regret it. So he went and did it. He got up from his chair, approached the girl and said those exact words. She laughed instantly and laughed for a while. Chad had this dumb smile on his face wondering what in the world he just said to have gotten that type of reaction. Just a refresher, Chad is that same big, heavyset dude I punched in the arm. So he finally asked her *what* those words meant, and she answered, "*Will you still love me even though I'm skinny?*" Chad swiveled his head around and stared at me as I laughed out loud. He wasn't angry afterwards, not really, and he did see the humor in it as I did.

Now you might be thinking that was a mean cruel joke I played on him, but do understand that I had the best of intentions. I am a firm believer that if you could make a girl laugh, you've won half the battle. I'm a big supporter of self-deprecating humor and I do it to myself all the time. I sincerely had Chad's best interest in mind. He didn't get made fun of or anything. The girl was a nice girl and really did think he was funny, but he just wasn't her type.

18. WINTER FORMAL COURT

*T*he first musical instrument I've ever taken lessons for was the accordion. It only lasted around half a year or so, but I grew a lot musically during that period. It became the key to understanding basic music theory, and it made it much easier to teach myself how to play the piano. It ultimately led to me picking up the alto sax and eventually joining the high school marching band. I've always been somewhat serious with my sax playing even when I just first started. I chose it because my dad's cousin Danny played it professionally, and I thought he was super cool. Danny was my very first inspiration to play the sax, and I wanted to be as good as he was. He gave me a few tips and explained to me how the blues scale worked.

I started learning how to play the sax at around the same time Kenny G became a global star. I instantly fell in love with his music when I heard "Silhouette" on the radio. It's one of the most beautiful songs ever written. I wanted to sound just like him. I didn't even have the proper saxophone as mine was an alto and Kenny G's main horn was the straight soprano sax. Now I just want to give a little bit of advice to all beginning to intermediate sax students out there. Kenny G is great; don't let any jazz snobs tell you otherwise. He may not be a traditional jazz player, but dude's got some serious chops and a lot of the crazy runs that he does are just as technical and complex as any jazz lick that ever came out of Charlie Parker's sax. But that wasn't the advice. My advice is, while it's okay to copy Kenny G's songs, don't stop there. Take sax lessons from a reputable pro. I did. It doesn't have to be anyone famous, just someone who's a professional. There are a lot of them out there and they will do wonders for your technique and musicianship.

So the whole Kenny G phenomenon lasted all throughout high school. It didn't matter whether or not you cared for his music, you still had to *recognize*. Now when I was in marching band, there was a hierarchy among the sax players as I'm sure there was among the other instruments. One of the few gifts I have is my musical ability. It didn't take too long for me to surpass the skill level of the older sax players in the marching band. I joined in the eighth grade and hung around until the 10th grade. I went through 3 different band directors. The third one wasn't very good. She just didn't have the kind of energy or vision that could inspire the whole band. The worst part about her was that she played favorites.

I was never a kiss up. I wanted to get the best saxophone parts based on my playing ability alone. There were two other sax players, both seniors, when I was a sophomore. I was much better than they were, but they were always given the best parts. That didn't sit well with me. I was *prideful*. I wasn't a Christian yet, and the most important thing to me was to glorify myself. I wanted my time in the spotlight and this band director didn't give me the opportunity. It was all about the two seniors. The marching band thinned out over the course of the year due to her overall incompetence. We were embarrassingly small by the end of the year and the band sounded pitiful.

With the two senior sax players graduating that year, this band director finally gave me the time of day and promised me the lead saxophone role for the upcoming year if I were to come back. I told her that I'd sign up, but then I didn't. I had no intention of signing up, but I've always been non-confrontational and I couldn't say no to her face. Plus the fact that I wasn't a Christian, I didn't feel too bad about lying to her. When the new schoolyear started, my junior year, she approached me and asked why I wasn't signed up for band. I simply played stupid and basically blamed a clerical error or something lame like that and walked away for good.

I quit marching band but I didn't quit playing my sax. I kept honing my skills and by the time I was a senior, I was pretty decent. I was good enough to provide the live saxophone music for the Winter Formal Court that was held at the gymnasium. As the court marched across the hardwood floor, my friend Ian (*that same Ian, you know, gazillionaire frenemy guy?*) and I played the background music. Ian was on the keyboard and I was on my soprano sax. I played a couple of Kenny G tunes, and for all intents and purposes, I sounded just like him. It was one of my favorite performances ever even though I wasn't the attraction. I kinda enjoy being in the background and doing my thing. The best part was that up in the bleachers was the marching band, consisting mostly of new people but with a few holdovers from when I was still part of it. Oh and, the same band director was up there with them. After the ceremonies one of her sax players came down to the floor to check out my sax and my equipment as the band director looked on. I was so in the flesh, just gloating. It was a little bit of revenge for never being given the respect I felt I deserved when I was still in her band. It felt great then, but it grieves me a little bit today when I think back. Had I been born again at that time, I'm not sure what I would've done or how I would've felt. At the very least I would've tried to make nice with her, let bygones be bygones, and maybe even apologized.

19. BAIT AND SWITCH

A week after my big "debut" saxophone performance in front of a live audience, which happened to be my entire high school, I had my first paid gig ever. I joined a party band, the kind that plays for uhm, *parties* and special occasions. Named, *"Main Course,"* they were mostly old geezers ranging from their late 20s to early 40s. I was 18, so yeah, they were old to me. The band played a mix of oldies, disco and some ballroom-style music including cha-cha, waltz, tango and "Achy Breaky Heart." My contribution was my Kenny G stuff. Saxophonists were a novelty, and a band with a sax soloist always made a good first impression. I played regularly with this band for around four years. We played at different venues, mostly hotels. The band wasn't very good, but when I started out with them, I was at their level and felt very fortunate to be able to play with a "real" band. I'd eventually surpass their level and would become more sensitive to their many, many flaws, but I won't get into that right now.

On my very first gig with them, which took place in a ballroom at the *Sequoia Health Club* in Buena Park, I saw one of the most beautiful girls I have ever seen in my entire life. Her name was Cheryl. My friend Darryl was with me that night and he's the only witness I have that I once met a girl who possessed such beauty. I told my friends about her and if you heard me talking, you'd think I was trying to convince my friends that I saw a *UFO* or the Loch Ness Monster (no, she didn't look like a Martian or a dinosaur). I first saw this girl when the band was just setting up. I saw her walk around the ballroom several times throughout the night. I was feeling it. My confidence was sky-high after performing a Kenny G song that was good enough for the guests to give me an honest round of applause.

In between sets, I decided to look for her, with my friend Darryl in tow. The entire place wasn't that big, and it didn't take long for me to find her. Now this was one of the few times that I actually went up to a girl who was a complete stranger to try to talk to her. As a matter of fact, off the top of my head, I could think of only four other occasions. So there she was, walking all by herself just being beautiful. I went for it. Darryl stayed back as I marched towards her. I introduced myself and asked what her name was, and she was kind enough to tell me. Now I don't know what the heck I was thinking, but the best thing I can come up with to get the conversation going was to tell her that my friend *Darryl wanted to meet her.* She looked briefly over my shoulder to take a quick glance, and we carried on with the conversation. Then I asked her if she wanted to take a short walk before it was time for the band to play again. As we started walking she asked, *"What about him?"* Darryl had no idea what I told Cheryl, but I waved at him to follow us. Now Darryl was a very handsome guy, and me, not so much. Cheryl was probably waiting for me to formally introduce the two of them to each other, but it never happened. Darryl just stayed back the whole time while Cheryl and I talked. I found out that she was our drummer's niece and that she had a boyfriend that she wasn't really thrilled to be with. *"He's really dead,"* were her exact words, and I had to ask Darryl afterwards what she could've possibly meant by that. She wasn't dating a deceased person, but rather one who was as boring as a dead guy. Cheryl was a very nice girl from an upper middle class family. She was respectful and had good manners even towards a loser like me who did a *bait and switch* on her. I approached her under the pretense of my friend wanting to talk to her and then entirely ditched the idea once *we* started talking to each other. I even had the audacity to ask for her phone number, which she surprisingly gave me.

Nothing ever became of us, never went on a date or anything. I'd see her on occasion at some family parties her uncle invited me to and sometimes she would be among the guests our band played for. We talked on the phone a few times and with each phone conversation it became more obvious that she wasn't the least bit into me. She rarely had any time to talk and always had a reason to have to hang up after a few short minutes. It was genuinely pathetic for me to have kept on pestering her. For me, it turned out to be a valuable experience in *rejection* and knowing when to say when. For a good three years she was my proverbial *Holy Grail*. I honestly can't tell you why I put myself through such indignity for such a long time. Cheryl never did or said anything that would ever suggest she was interested in me, well except maybe once, which I'll talk about later. I was just a complete fool who refused to accept reality.

20. OOH ECHO

*M*y second gig with *Main Course* took place exactly four weeks later. I believe it was for a wedding reception. It was a nice venue, very classy. The place was packed. I was looking forward to playing on stage because it was still very novel to me, but I was still a bit nervous. These days I don't really have stage fright because I haven't had too many opportunities to play in front of people. But seriously, when I'm playing my sax I feel like I'm in my element. Over the years I've learned to tune out the audience so that I can just concentrate on putting my heart and soul behind every note that comes out of my horn. I've improved significantly from the days I first started playing in public, when I was barely over 18. My enhanced skills combined with more maturity and simply developing the ability to not care so much about what others think has all but eliminated every last ounce of stage fright I had in me. I still get butterflies in my stomach before I start playing, but they're good butterflies, like I can't wait to share my music with these people.

It's funny how it's necessary *to tune out* the audience, to be able to play to the best of my ability so that I can make that connection *with the audience*. But that's how it works. If you think too much about whether or not they'll like your music, actually no, if you think about it *at all*, you will *surely* hinder your performance. Such was the case on my second gig with Main Course. I couldn't have been more self-conscious, and that's the last thing I needed to be. Part of it had to do with the guests, who were more than a little pompous. You can sense these things even if you can't explain why. Groups of people are just as unique as individual humans. I came to understand that more clearly every time I performed with Main Course. I eventually got to a point where hundreds of people together seemed like one living organism to me. This particular one was just a giant *jerk*. It was one of my worst performances. I was hitting wrong notes and I think my horn may have squeaked a couple of times as well. I was *dying* on stage as I played one of Kenny G's songs. My misfortune was that I usually played while people were still eating at their tables. That meant the audience were more inclined to watch and pay attention to the performers on stage. My favorite part of every gig was when the guests were on the dance floor having a good time. It was freedom for me to just improvise on my sax and go with the flow.

Whenever I was playing Kenny G, however, it was the complete opposite. Kenny G is essentially his own genre of music. When you play a Kenny G song on your sax, you have to do every little thing that he does, note for note, at least as much as you're capable of doing. It's not much different from walking on a tight rope. On this gig, I more or less fell to my death. To make matters worse, the reverb on my saxophone wasn't hooked up properly. Reverb does wonders to vocals. It masks a lot of flaws and imperfections. Even for great singers, reverb is needed to make their voice blend properly with the overall sound of the band. The same is true for the saxophone. There must've been a loose connection on the mixer. It made me sound worse. During the middle of my playing one of the band members finally figured out what was wrong and got the reverb flowing through my mic instantly. At that very moment I heard this jerk guy in the audience mockingly say to his buddy, *"Ooh, echo!"* I've been noticing the two of them snicker throughout my solo, but up until that moment I figured they could've been talking about anything, even though they've been staring at me. Then my reverb kicked in, immediately followed by their, *"Ooh, echo!"* and I knew beyond a doubt they've been making fun of me. That was one of the most embarrassing moments of my life. It wasn't as though they yelled it out loud, they just sat close enough to the stage for me to hear.

The majority of my most humiliating moments are tied to my saxophone playing in some way, shape or form. It's likely because I put so much of myself into my music that the sense of failure is greatly enhanced. For the longest time, my music was the main fiber of my being. That was me, the sax player. Before I was anything else, I identified as a saxophonist. Eventually when I got saved, my new identity became Christ, and I started seeing my musical gift as a way to bring honor and glory to Jesus rather than myself.

21. THE FIX

Cheryl became my ultimate romantic conquest. She had the looks and personality that I was drawn to. She was soft spoken, almost shy, but you could tell she was quite sure of herself. I've observed her interaction with others and liked what I saw. She's straight out of a romantic teen movie. Think of a story where the high school star quarterback goes around knowing that all the girls want him. He's the class king and everyone bows down. But there's this *one* girl, just as hot as all the cheerleaders. She views herself as plain and prefers to keep a low profile. She also doesn't care one bit about the quarterback's massive deltoids or epic jaw line. Instead she falls for some loner who turns out to be the greatest guy ever even though everyone else thinks he's a loser. That's how I perceived Cheryl. And yes, I gladly designated myself as "the loser." If there's anything I've learned from the movies, it's that a million to one shot means *I have chance.*

Now Cheryl being Main Course drummer's niece, I saw her quite often. They were a big, tight-knit family and the drummer treated the band like family. We were often invited to their family events, and half the time Cheryl would be there. Her dad and my dad even met each other during one of these occasions. My dad had heard of Cheryl before as word got around fast. For my dad to finally see Cheryl in person was indeed a treat for him. He was quite impressed with my choice, but probably not with my chances. At any rate, my dad and Cheryl's dad seemed to hit it off, which to me was a good sign. The foundations were being laid, one brick at a time. If her dad was welcoming to my dad, it could only mean that he considered me a *worthy suitor.* Better yet, perhaps he knew something I didn't, that Cheryl was more into me than she let on. Forget that she hardly ever acknowledged my presence and forget the fact that she had turned me down *every single time* I called to ask if I could see her. Her dad and my dad were *cool.*

It would only be a matter of time. *I was in there like swimwear.*

So there was this big party that her family threw at some fancy ballroom. I'm pretty sure it was for the drummer's daughter's eighteenth birthday. Naturally, *Main Course* would provide all the music for the night. Cheryl was there, of course. Whenever I knew she was going to attend an event our band was playing at, I got energized. Every note that came out of my sax would be directed at her, like Cupid's arrows. On that night I played with more passion than the band was used to seeing from me. After one of our sets, as I was setting my saxophone on its stand, I was approached by none other than Cheryl. She rested her arms on the stage as she looked up at me. She smiled and said, *"I just came to see your work."* I don't remember what we said to each other after, but it was a pleasant exchange that felt glorious for the entire two minutes it lasted. It was the first time she has ever come up to me to strike up a conversation. I was on cloud nine. She was coming around, I thought, most likely tired of playing *hard to get.* Perhaps one of the notes I shot out of my sax hit the *bullseye* on her heart. Whatever it was, things were finally looking up and my patience and persistence were beginning to pay off. At the end of the night, when most of the guests had left and the band was packing up, the drummer's wife teased me and commented on how *girls were now chasing me.* It was a good night. I was beginning to win Cheryl over and her family was totally cool with it.

Now if you've been reading this book in order, then you already know that I got *nowhere* with Cheryl. So what was this night all about? As it turns out, Cheryl's dad was selling some multi-level marketing thing to my dad. I think it may have been Excel Communications. My dad ended up buying it, whatever it was that he had to buy. My dad basically did it to improve my chances with Cheryl. Cheryl did what she did to help her dad sell to my dad. She was merely following instructions. The fix was in from the get-go. They were all in on it, including the drummer's wife. It was pretty dishonorable. I didn't actually see it that way until many years later because as they say, love is blind. Like I said before, I was a complete fool. Oh, and by the way, the last time I saw Cheryl, she was with a guy who had a pretty epic jawline.

22. GREAT AS ALWAYS

I've always been musically talented. I'm by no means a prodigy, not even close. But music is an actual gift that I have. I have a natural artistry when it comes to musical expression. For the first several years of my saxophone playing, all I went on was *natural talent*. I had no technical practice routine to speak of. My "practice" basically consisted of playing along with my favorite songs. Any real musician knows that that's *not* going to cut it. In order to improve, you need to practice. Playing along with songs does not count as practice. Practice is discipline and dedication to play the boring scales and various exercises that focus on technique and the *physicality* of playing your instrument. It's the mundane repetition that develops a sax player's tone quality and finger dexterity. Acquiring that "saxophone sound" is one of the most difficult things to achieve. Anybody can press a piano key or even several keys at once to form a chord, and it will come out sounding like a piano. But someone who has never played the saxophone can't simply blow into a sax and expect to produce any sound, let alone that classic, cool saxophone sound.

It takes years to achieve the unique, unmistakable sound of a saxophone, and it takes just as long to develop the minimum technical proficiency needed to be considered a *"functional"* sax player who is able to sit down and play under most musical conditions. I did manage to achieve that much. Now I can't improvise like the top jazz musicians, but I can hold my own improvising "smooth jazz," considered by elitists to be inferior to "real" jazz. It doesn't matter to me. I love improvising because it's *freedom*. It's the complete opposite of having to be tied down to the notes written on a sheet of paper. I liken playing jazz (or smooth jazz) to being *born again*. In contrast, *religion* is the equivalent of being required to play the most complicated classical piece without making a single error. Religious people who believe that salvation is earned through works always get upset when I tell them that we are *saved by grace through faith*. They'll often come back with something like, "*If you're saved by grace, then why don't you just go around sinning and run amok, since you'll go to heaven no matter what?*" I would then explain to them that being born again means you are a new creation in Christ and therefore have a new nature. A (smooth) jazz musician who improvises and plays "*whatever he wants*," does so to make the most beautiful music he can come up with on the spot. Without the requirement of having to stick to printed notes on paper, he is able to play *from his heart*. He's not trying to play as terribly as he possibly could. In fact, it's quite the opposite. The same thing goes for the Christian. We're no longer under the Law, but we live to please the Lord the best we possibly can, because that's the new nature we have in us. Grace is not a license for us to sin as much as we want, *but empowerment for us to serve the Lord.*

As for my saxophone skills, I didn't improve much until I started taking lessons from a world renowned saxophonist. I won't mention his name, but he's not a famous saxophonist. He is well respected and highly regarded by jazz musicians and definitely among the best of the best, but unless you're really into jazz or smooth jazz, you probably have never heard of him. I took many lessons from him. When all was said done, I walked away with two things. First and foremost was *technique*. He taught me how to practice properly. Once he instilled that in me, it didn't take long for my skills to go through the roof. Second and just as important was that he gave me *confidence* in my abilities. Part of our lesson routine was me and him taking turns improvising over a pre-recorded track. He would shred me to pieces during this part of the lesson, but it gave me the confidence that since I could hang with him, even if just barely, I could play with *most* musicians.

By now you know that I played with a copies band called *Main Course* for about four years. It was actually more like three years because we basically disbanded after that, but we did get together a little over a year later for one last gig. During that gap was when I made the biggest improvement. I don't remember what the gig was for, but it was another one of those fancy parties held at some hotel. I killed it that night. I sounded *like* a pro. I received compliments from guests who had heard me play in the past, noting my improvement. By this time I was already a Christian and I didn't let it get to my head, but I did appreciate the kind words. However, there was this one guy who was a family friend to one of the band members. He's what you would call a hater. *Extremely* insecure. At the end of the night he came up to me and said, "*You were great as always*!" Fair enough, gracious words. Then he followed it up with, "*No change!*" I got it. I knew exactly what he was trying to do, but I didn't let it bother me. In fact, a grin formed on my face involuntarily as soon as those words came out of his mouth. It was confirmation that my hard work had paid off, and that I'd taken my sax playing to the next level. I kind of felt sorry for him actually.

23. ONE-PUNCHED MAN

I can't boast of ever being in a fist fight, let alone winning one. I've said before that street fights make no sense whatsoever, and I stand by that. If you're cool-headed enough to fight in a tactical, calculated manner, then you're cool enough to walk away from it. Guys who get in fights without getting paid for it are idiots. That does not mean that I don't wish that I could've gotten in a scrap or two during high school. It would've been the perfect time in anyone's life. You've got a kid's brain inside the body of an adult. It's the best of times. You've got the resiliency to take a beating and keep on ticking, consequences be damned. Why not go for it, right? Times were different when I was a teenager. They were already pretty bad, don't get me wrong. I grew up listening to many versions of *"when I was your age"* stories, told by older men and women, describing how *innocent* their generation was. Now you get to hear *my* version. My generation was *not* innocent. In fact I can recall as early as age 10, hearing some of the most depraved words coming out of the mouths of my peers. It was indeed shocking to me.

As a teenager things were even worse. There were gangs. I'm sure they've been around long before my time, but gangs were sensationalized when I was growing up. They were the hot topic in the news. Drive-by shootings, people getting *jumped*, and drugs. Their existence made people uneasy, mostly adults. Kids, on the other hand, revered the *idea* of grown men roaming the streets in packs, doing whatever they pleased, seemingly *untouchable*. Kids saw their defiance as *power*. However gangs weren't the only thing. There was everything else. Drug use was common. I've never known a coke or heroin addict, but at least two of my friends smoked marijuana. Also, girls got pregnant in high school. A handful of pregnancies made the headlines during my junior and senior years, and they really were a big deal. Interestingly, abortion wasn't as big then. When you hear about someone getting pregnant, it was more or less a given that you'll see their tummy get bigger and bigger throughout the schoolyear. Some will simply drop out of school to take on their new role as a mother. Not only was abortion *not* considered the obvious and logical "*solution*" to a pregnancy, it was still generally frowned upon by the society I grew up in. It certainly wasn't the casual subject it has become today, where young women discuss their abortions as though they were merely talking about their new *tattoos*. So I guess in this sense, things were pretty innocent when I was a teenager. Yes, you have the rebellious types who didn't care about rules or the society's norms, but in those days, the general population still had a little bit of shame left. Their dark deeds were kept in secret, not flaunted in broad daylight.

Furthermore, your typical fist fight had some honor left. When two guys went at it, it was settled. Maybe they'll hate each other and punch each other in the face at every chance they got, but it was always just a fight. How I sometimes wish I would've gotten the opportunity to truly put my boxing skills to the test! I never disliked any guy in high school, at least not to the point of wanting to break his face. I'm really one of the most laid back guys you could ever meet. I just find physical confrontation silly, unless you're doing it for self-defense. I wouldn't want to get into a fist fight today as a younger man or otherwise. The world has just gotten so bad over the past twenty years. I'm genuinely afraid of people who are unsaved knowing what they are capable of doing. They literally have no boundaries. Even real Christians are capable of the most heinous acts given the right circumstances. How much worse can be said of an unbeliever who does not have the presence of the Holy Spirit in their life? If you won a street fight today, there's no telling if that's the end. I mean, it could be, but there's a better chance of the guy you beat up coming back some other time with a deadly weapon. People today have no remorse. They are lovers of self and unapologetically violent. They will stop at almost nothing when driven by desire to do whatever. We are seeing Bible prophecy unfold right before our very eyes.

When I was 18, people weren't quite like that. Sometimes there doesn't even have to be a fight. A single blow to the head could be sufficient to settle a wrong, for good, depending on the punch and depending on the head. There was this guy named George who was treated like an outcast for most of high school. He was a loner, had weird mannerisms, and wasn't the most physically gifted. He was a lanky fellow. Think of the original *Karate Kid* but without the karate. That would be George, and not nearly as cool. He was *fodder*. He got picked on but lucky for him, never physically. He was also incredibly smart. I believe he graduated as the number two guy in our class. I'm not exactly sure what he does today, but the guy's pretty loaded. Even more loaded than the backpack he used to wear on his back pretty much wherever he went. He kept it on like a parachute.

One day while George and I were chatting right outside of class, for whatever reason, I gave him a little nudge on his shoulder. There was no ill intent whatsoever, but neither his puny physique nor gravity cares about intentions. With a backpack that probably weighed as much as he did, it didn't take much force. He fell like a tree. And I do mean like a tree. It wasn't like he lost his balance and tried to stay upright before falling on his butt. No, his body remained straight and stiff as he fell backwards and landed on his backpack. What I did not expect to see was George getting back up in a hurry, winding up the wimpiest punch you could imagine and hurling his fist at my head. Now you have to understand that I have naturally fast reflexes. Even today, as a middle-aged man, I'm quite adept at parrying and picking off punches. If I see a hand coming towards my face, I instinctively would deflect it even if the other person meant no harm whatsoever. But on that particular moment, with George's fist loaded with the baddest of intentions, my brain made quick assessment of the situation and found the threat level to be at zero. My reflexes did not engage, but instead my amusement. It was the most awkward and sloppiest punch I have ever seen, devoid of any critical velocity. So I literally stood there and watched his fist travel on the most inefficient trajectory until it landed squarely on my forehead with the softest "thump." I burst out laughing immediately after. George didn't feel the need to follow it up with another punch. As far as he's concerned, I got my *comeuppance*. He cooled off pretty fast after and cracked a smile. So yeah, I've never been in a fight and I've never punched anyone in the face. But for some twisted reason, I'm actually very fond of this incident. George punched me in the head. To this day he remains the only man to have ever had the privilege. I hope he feels blessed.

PART 3: COLLEGE

*D*iscovering yourself; expanding your horizons; frat parties; forming lifelong friendships—that's what college is all about. I didn't get any of that during college. I did not make a single friend in college. Not one. I did get saved during my college years, but college really had nothing to do with it and I'll talk more about that soon. My college experience is characterized by the complete absence of direction. I was lost. I didn't see the point or purpose behind it. I had all these strange ideas in my head on what college was supposed to do to me and for me. None of it truly made sense to me. I was too stupid to understand the big picture. I didn't know how it would work and how it would benefit me for the rest of my life. I did not finish college. It's one of the biggest regrets of my life. I only wish I had better guidance to help me focus and understand what college was really for. It would've greatly helped me through the worst slogs.

I attended Cal State Long Beach for nearly 5 years before dropping out. I wasn't in college all 5 years; there was about a year and a half gap during which I had to work full time. But the reality of it is that I mentally checked out long before I stopped going for good. There were numerous occasions where I would skip class and just hang out with my best friend from high school. I didn't care if I flunked classes. I believe I reached that point maybe sometime during my third year. The first two years of college were okay. At least I was passing my classes. Then classes became a little more challenging and since I had zero passion for them, I didn't bother trying. I picked my major based on what I thought would be practical rather than what I was interested in. Probably one of the biggest mistakes anyone can make. You need to be interested in what you're doing. It's the only thing that will push you when things get super boring or super difficult, which for most students it will at some point. You've got to have a prize to keep your eye on.

With no prize in sight, you just want it to be over. Why wait till the very end when there's nothing there waiting for you? That's basically what happened.

I have no college stories or adventures, at least not triumphant ones. No, college was pretty uneventful for me. A little over a year after I dropped out of Cal State Long Beach, I did go back to a community college to major in music for a couple of semesters. I didn't really have a plan. I was past the age by which most students graduated college. I had no financial means to see my second stint all the way through to the end. I basically did it for fun. I felt old, because I *was* old. It felt like a bad dream, really. I had already been working full time and it felt like a major step backwards to start over at 24, with most of my classmates being freshmen who were barely over 18. It only helped remind me that I had failed and wasted my opportunities. I should've had a career by then, but instead there I was pretending to be a student with a bright future. It was as though I did it just to get a taste of what it would've been like to start college knowing what I wanted. Boy, did it taste great. Why didn't I have this figured out six years prior? The simple answer is that I was just *that* stupid.

I hate to bring my parents up again, but they sheltered me so aggressively during high school that when I finally was placed in an environment without the shackles of high school, I couldn't handle the freedom with any responsibility. In college, there weren't any bells to signify it was time to go to class. Students didn't get sent to the vice principal's office for misbehaving in class. Students *didn't* misbehave in class. College treats you like an adult because you technical are. Missing class or not paying attention to the lectures didn't mean the professor was going to call your parents. No, it had *real* consequences. You pay several hundred dollars for just one class in a semester. If you choose to not show up then it's your loss. Not only is it money down the drain, it's your friggin' future. Like, literally. I wish I had understood that then. Nothing remarkable happened to me *in* college. There were some mildly amusing things that I went through *during* college, which is what I'll be writing about in this section. I do hope that you find them entertaining enough.

1. COULD'VE BEEN A CONTENDER

*B*oxing was my favorite sport growing up. It was my passion. I loved watching boxing matches and boxing movies. I loved pretending to be a boxer. I made my action figures box each other. When I was around 15, my uncle gave me some valuable pointers in boxing fundamentals. He showed me some basic footwork and taught me how to throw "real" punches. He showed me punch combinations that I could practice on my heavy bag and he taught me how to properly wrap my hands. Using hand wraps, now *that's* what separated the men from the boys. That was *serious* stuff. That instantly elevated me from being some wannabe to *a serious student of the sweet science* (Alliteration, yay!!!).

You see, I wasn't just some punk kid messing around on a punching bag not knowing what he was doing. No, I was a promising young talent who's about to put some real hurt on the punching bag. The punches I was about to throw were no joke. They were *deadly*. But that goes both ways. My fists, the tools of my trade, could potentially get damaged by the incredible impact. I must protect my weapons of destruction. A lot of the great ones broke their hands at some point. I knew that I would inevitably suffer the same fate, but I will save it for the boxing ring, for one of my career-defining bouts in which I will break my hand early on and still emerge victorious. Wrapping your hands became almost ritualistic for me. The two minutes it took to do both hands were also spent imagining glorious sequences of landing the most amazing combinations on a worthy foe who ultimately was no match for my otherworldly boxing skills.

Hitting the bag became a regular part of whatever kind of workout I had in my mid to late teens. I took it a notch higher. I may have been 16 or 17, and I don't know how it even came about, but I joined a real boxing gym in Pasadena. My dad drove me there a few times. It was a bit of a drive from Orange County. It was a small, hole in the wall type of gym, but it was *authentic*. The gym consisted of a bunch of nobody's with professional experience. They went there because they loved their sport. I knew enough about boxing to know that these were no-hopers. They just loved the idea of coming to a boxing gym to do some boxing exercises and some light sparring. From time to time there would be some visitors who were a little more ambitious than the regulars. They'd show up to basically gauge themselves by sparring with one of the better guys in the gym. The sparring would get just a tiny bit heated at times, but never out of hand. I never got to spar. I wasn't physically ready for it.

The main coach wanted me to work on hardening my abdominals before he would let me spar. He made me feel his abs to give me an idea of where I should be at. Now this guy was in his mid-40s at least and he wasn't in the best of shape, but his abs felt rock solid to me. You knew that he'd been doing this for many, many years. He showed me a few ab exercises I could do on my own time. I wasn't able to harden my abs enough to spar during my time at that gym, but I did get to step inside the ring to hit the mitts. I learned combinations and how to move my head properly. It felt amazing to be doing the kind of drills I used to only see on TV, especially with a real boxing coach. The coach was truly impressed with my form and technique. He saw real potential in me. You could tell that wheels were turning in his head. I remember one particular look he gave me, like he was making an assessment. He was standing next to another coach and he said to me, "*You're a little bigger than Carbajal.*" Then he turned his head to the other guy and said, "*He's a little bigger than Carbajal.*" He was referring to Michael Carbajal, who at the time was one of the most popular flyweights. He fought with an intense, aggressive style that drew comparisons to the great Roberto Duran. I don't know what the coach was thinking. Perhaps he was seeing a potential showdown between me and Carbajal down the road? At any rate, this all fizzled out, I stopped going to the gym and life went on.

A couple of years went by and one afternoon, as I stood in the middle of the living room shadowboxing, I bragged to my parents about my form. My mom looked at my dad and they had this look on their faces. Then my mom said to me, *"You know, we never told you this, but that gym you used to go to wanted to train you to become a professional boxer."* I was like, "What?" She confessed that she intercepted a letter from the gym, which stated their intent to develop me into a real boxer. She said that when she saw the envelope she sensed *something* was up. And just like any mother who didn't give a crap about her son's privacy, she opened it, read it, showed my dad and got rid of it *forever*.

Now at that point I really didn't care that she did that. It had been at least two years and as much as I loved boxing, I knew I didn't really have it in me to fully dedicate myself to becoming a professional boxer. There were so many sacrifices required that, frankly, I was not willing to make for something so uncertain. Also, I knew I wasn't tough enough. I could work on my ab muscles and make them as hard as a brick wall and I could work on my cardio so that I could throw a hundred punches per round for 12 rounds. But I couldn't work on my ability to take a full punch to the chin. Yes, there are some things you can do to help with that, like developing your neck muscles, but the ability to take a punch to the face is something one is born with. You're either tough or you ain't. And trust me, *I ain't*. If ever I got caught flush on the jaw with a decent punch from a professional, I would certainly go down. If it hit me just right, heck, I may never get back up.

So no, I wasn't disappointed that my mom denied me an opportunity. I was more upset that she got into my stuff. But I was even more flattered by the fact that a professional boxing coach saw something in me that for years I only imagined to have. Perhaps I could've been a contender. Maybe even a champ. I wasn't tough but there's no law that says I have to get hit. I could work on my defense. When all was said and done, I was left with a bunch of *"what ifs."* But I was perfectly content with those.

2. ALONG CAME HOLLY

*S*hortly after I graduated from high school, I became determined to break out of my shell and start taking chances—with girls. By "chances" I mean to try talking to them, something I didn't really do in high school. I don't think I ever asked anybody out, not in a straightforward way, anyway. I mean I sent notes to a couple of girls, I think, and there was Marissa, who actually went places with me, but I never just straight up told any girl how I felt about them. I was afraid of the rejection and the humiliation that would follow once everyone else heard about it. If I could go back in time that's most certainly one of the things I would've done differently. I would've just gone for it, looked rejection in the eye and laughed afterwards. At the very least I would've just walked up to the girls I was interested in and struck up a conversation. You know, like a normal human being. And if they gave me a dirty look or made a fuss about it, then that would've been on *them*. I would hold my head up high even if the guys started making fun of me for getting turned down by a girl. I was a little bolder during my junior and senior years, but still not nearly as daring as I wish I would've been.

When I started college, I vowed to take more chances and be more outgoing and see where it took me. To me college was a clean slate. I didn't have a history with anybody, and my classmates would have to take me at *face value* rather than the reputation I earned over the years. As it turned out, it didn't make much of a difference. Everywhere I looked, students were already grouped together. They were probably not freshmen, but I couldn't help feeling a little discouraged. Not that I was expecting every single classmate to fall down at my feet and beg me to be their friend, but I really thought that everyone would be a lot more social. I was kinda hoping to see a bunch of wide-eyed freshmen just looking around waiting to make eye contact with *anyone* and be ever so willing to introduce themselves and have lunch together at the student union. No, it wasn't like that. Most students kept to themselves and were caught in their own little world. And this was a good two decades before everybody had *smartphones* and didn't have the need to acknowledge the presence of anyone around them.

On my very first day in college, *I talked to a girl*. I didn't hit on her or anything. I was done with school for the day just walking around in the parking lot headed to my car. Now Cal State Long Beach's parking lot was insanely *packed*. Depending on the time of day you came, you may or may not find a parking space. So there was this girl who was driving around looking for parking, and she rolled down her window to ask me if I was leaving, and if she could take my parking space. She was pretty cute, so naturally I said yes. We drove around for a minute and when we got to my car, I mustered up the courage to ask for her name. It was *"Yasmine."* Now I didn't ask for her phone number or anything, she looked older than me anyway. But for me it was a great start, *talking to a female* on my very first day.

Fast forward a semester and there was this cute blonde girl in my philosophy class. She was quiet, which was always a plus to me. I always found loud, outspoken girls unattractive. Perhaps I was just intimidated by them. I liked girls who kept to themselves and didn't want to be the center of attention all the time. This girl fit the bill. Her name was Holly. I don't remember if I had introduced myself to her or just knew her name because I heard the professor say it. I don't remember how often I talked to her or what we talked about. Whatever kind of conversations we had, they were the equivalent of a left jab in boxing. I was merely finding the range and setting up my right hand. I did my best to not come across as some guy with any hidden intentions. I was just being *casual normal friendly*. That's how naïve I was. Every girl who wasn't born yesterday knows that there is no such thing as "casual normal friendly." Ninety percent of the time when a guy tries to talk to a girl, it's *because he's interested*. It's fairly obvious when a guy is just looking for any reason to talk to a girl. I was *that guy* to Holly.

One day immediately after class, Holly met up with some guy who was waiting for her and they started walking together. I don't know if it was a boyfriend or not, but they were clearly well acquainted with each other. I walked not too far behind them, maybe 10 to 15 yards at the most, going towards the same direction. Suddenly, Holly looked over her shoulder and glanced at me for a second. Then the guy turned around with a smile on his face and looked at me as well. After that they just kept on walking and went about their business. The whole incident lasted maybe 5 seconds but it felt intensely embarrassing. I knew exactly what it was about and I felt *deflated*. It was so subtle and yet managed to pierce me pretty deeply. It was as though reality had just come back from vacation and pounded on my door.

3. FORBIDDEN LOVE

I'm not going to beat around the bush about this one. I'm well aware of my writing tendencies in this book. I'd go round and round until I make it to the actual topic. I honestly didn't plan it out that way. It just sort of happened that way naturally. I began to notice the pattern a few stories in. I'm kinda doing it again right now. But I'll cut to the chase. When I was 19, I fell in love with my first cousin. There. I said it. Let's just call her *"Marsha."* And before I say anything else, I want to make it clear that *nothing* physical ever happened between us. So what did happen? She and her family came to visit us from Canada. They stayed with us for about a week. The last time I saw her was 10 years prior, when she was just this dorky, short-haired girl. But when she set foot inside our house on that first night, I saw a stunningly beautiful young woman with long, flowing black hair. Yes, I know, I know. It's not among my proudest moments. I do find it all amusing because, well, just because.

It's easy for me to look back as I'm not the same person anymore. And oh, by the way, I was not a Christian yet. It'd be about another year or so before I would get saved, but I'll tell you more about that later. The point is, as a non-Christian, I had even less defenses against Marsha's charms. She came with her parents and her older sisters, who treated me like their younger brother. Marsha and I were never really playmates as little kids. We sorta just ignored each other when we were both tiny. So when I gazed upon her beauty that fateful night, it was as though we just met for the very first time. It took a couple of days for us to warm up to each other. Our families spent a lot of time hanging out together, going to a bunch of places including Universal Studios and Las Vegas. Marsha and I were playful towards each other, borderline flirtatious. We got *really* close. I fell for her *hard*. I felt like I was in a magic spell. Besides her otherworldly beauty, a big part of the reason was that I have never experienced a friendship like this with any girl. We were so open about everything and we could talk about anything. Truth be told, it could've been Chewbacca's sister and I probably would've fallen in love just as badly. At that point of my life I had never experienced such emotional intimacy. It was *intoxicating*. Marsha and I truly bonded during that week. She was in tears when we hugged goodbye at LAX. I wish I could say that that was the end of it, but it wasn't.

About a week later, my dad and I flew to Canada to visit them. They invited us and we had the money, so my dad accepted. Technically, we flew to Seattle and drove the rest of the way to their home in Richmond, British Columbia, where my dad and I would stay. I had every intention to profess my love for her during our stay. A couple of days before my dad and I left for Canada, I talked to a priest over the phone in secret to ask him if it was permissible to marry one's cousin. I didn't get a straight answer. I also didn't get a negative answer, and that was all the empowerment I needed to go on my *quest*. So we got to Richmond, and Marsha and I were pretty inseparable. We hung out with each other the entire time, watched movies and played video games together. We even slept together. As in *literally sleeping*. We fell asleep right next to each other on the living room floor after watching a movie late into the night. Then on one afternoon we took a nap together *on her bed*. What was more important was on that same morning, I took my shot. I professed my love for her. I wrote it on a small piece of paper. *"I'm in love with you."* She read it, crumpled it and didn't say anything. I honestly couldn't tell you how she felt. She still didn't mind taking a nap with me later that day so I'm thinking she may have felt the same way, at least a little. The interesting thing was that nobody seemed to notice what was going on between us; not even my dad. Even after I told her how I felt, it didn't get too weird. We still treated each other the same the rest of the time.

Now my dad and I were supposed to stay an entire week, but we left a couple of days early. Then came the long distance calls. I believe I talked to her on the phone the very next night. She cried over the phone saying that I should still be there with her in Canada. For the next three weeks we would talk to each other on the phone for several hours each night. I ran up our phone bill *big time*. I think it was over $700, maybe more. I don't remember exactly how the whole thing fizzled out. Maybe it was the phone bill. I simply couldn't call Canada anymore. My parents were not happy. It was for the best.

Marsha never really told me straight up that she liked me the same way I liked her, but at the same time she never flat out rejected me. It would've been easy to do even in a nice way. *"We're related. We can't do this."* Or something like that. No, she just sort of went with it. So this episode lasted maybe four or five weeks. It was intense. I can't believe I actually got over her at the time, when I was the least equipped to deal with *anything*.

4. BAND CAMP

My first real experience playing with world class musicians was "Berklee in L.A." It was a week-long band camp held at Claremont McKenna College, hosted by the world famous Berklee College of Music. It was specifically geared toward aspiring jazz musicians of all levels. It was one of the most unforgettable times of my life. Simply being around students of all ages who were interested in the same music that I loved to play was an amazing experience. Well, technically I'm not a jazz man, more like a smooth jazz man. I was 20 years old, and at that point I had been playing the sax for over seven years. My development during those years was less than ideal. I was mostly getting by on natural talent and without any discipline to practice. I didn't know how. I had a fairly good sax tone and I could play expressively, but my improvisation skills were lacking. They are still lacking today, but not nearly as much.

I wasn't horrible, even with my limited abilities. At least I could pick the right notes to play even if I couldn't utilize as many notes as the better players could. I wasn't *tone deaf*. There were some pretty lousy players in that camp. I wasn't one of them. At that time, my biggest influence was Kenny G, and I was proud of it. It was the first time I was jeered for emulating him. Actually, it may have been the only time in my life, but that was enough. I learned firsthand that jazz students didn't think much of Kenny G. The students weren't mean spirited, they were just teasing me in good fun, and I got it. There were some pretty awesome sax players there who were capable of playing "real" jazz, but they admitted that it was important for them to be able to bust out some Kenny G tunes for parties and such. It was all good.

The camp opened my eyes to what's out there and how *competitive* the music industry is. In spite of my limitations, I was still a bit *smug*. By the way, I wasn't a Christian yet, just to let you know. Now, I didn't think that I was better than everybody, and I definitely wasn't the best saxophonist, but I was better than *a lot* of the sax players there. Also, the camp was for all instruments, not just saxes. There were trumpets, guitars, keyboards, flutes, bass, drums, you name it. My favorite part of camp was not the classes, but the jam sessions that took place in the evenings. There were several setups outside the dorm rooms and students could just walk around with their instruments and jump in. During the day we attended various clinics that focus on different aspects of jazz, just basic stuff, really. After the classes, students were broken up into different bands to learn a few songs to perform for the concert scheduled on the last day. It was band camp after all.

There were so many different personalities. I was cool enough to not draw any special attention to myself, and I was happy with that. Some were not quite so lucky. I remember one specific guy, another sax player, who was likely in his mid-50s and was barely over a beginner. It's a jazz camp for all levels, remember? The guy truly sucked. He was clueless and was in his own little world. Students were respectful and didn't try to make fun of him or anything like that. The guy was *trying*, I give him that, but he just didn't have a musical bone in his body. His tone was horrible, his sight reading was barely passable, and he couldn't *improvise*. He *honked*. That's what he did with his sax. He *honked* like a goose. Now this guy was probably some rich, successful man. You know the type. He's got it all together and is set for life but wants to try new things to conquer, like *playing the saxophone*. Every rehearsal he messed up in some fashion. I found it entertaining. By now you should know that I'm a prankster at heart. It's just who I am. I don't prank people to make them feel bad, but to bring them to the place where they can laugh at themselves, which I think is liberating. I almost always have good intentions.

Well, I didn't really have time to pull a prank on anyone, but there was this tricky part in one of the songs we were rehearsing. This being a jazz camp and all, every song we learned featured a brief solo from some of the better musicians in the group. I was among those musicians. To be honest, I wasn't looking forward to my solo because during this stage of my life, I simply wasn't good enough to improvise over the kind of songs we were learning. They were the old fashioned, traditional jazz stuff. Those are the hardest styles to improvise over and I didn't have the skills. So anyway, back to the tricky part of the song. There was an awkward *rest* (it's essentially a "pause" in the music, for all you guys who may not have any musical background) followed by a short jazz lick by the sax section. The timing for that first note was a real *doozy*. You had to be tapping your toes and counting in your head to get it right. I knew that this guy was struggling so I did the thing most people in my situation would've done; I "guided" him by taking a big breath to indicate I was about to blow into my horn, raised my sax during the upbeat and brought it down hard on the downbeat. It was the musical version of *"on your mark, get set, go!"* The downbeat was the "go" part, and I deliberately did the whole gesture with the wrong timing. It resulted in a false start for the guy, honking out the note about 4 counts too early. Some of the sax players chuckled quietly. The band director definitely noticed what I did but didn't do anything about it *then*.

On the last day of camp, during the concert, when it was my turn to solo, the band director skipped me. You see, the soloists were supposed to watch for the band director's signal before they could jump in to do their solo even though we all knew the order of each solo. When it was nearing my turn I kept my eyes glued at him. He briefly looked at me and then turned his head towards the guy who was supposed to solo after me, and gave him the green light. I deserved it. I truly did. I was embarrassed inside, even though when I think of it today, I'm not sure whether or not I'd have been as embarrassed had I been allowed to solo that day.

5. TV STAR

I got my driver's license when I was 16 years old, like most teenagers did in California. But I didn't get a car until my senior year of high school. My very first car was a 1986 Toyota Supra. It remains to this very day, my favorite of all the cars I've ever owned. It was actually quite impressive to have one in high school. It was arguably the best car any student had at my school. I had that car for nearly seven years before I totaled it. I'll share the details in another story. When I first got my license, as in the first few years, I was afraid to go on the freeway. It was a little terrifying for me. It was chaos. The freeways in California are probably among the craziest in the country. There are lots of cars, lots of lanes and lots of freeways coming together. I would discover later in life, however, how impressively organized and thought out the freeway system in California is compared to other parts of the country, where the freeways don't make sense.

It took me a good two years to overcome my phobia of driving on freeways. It started on one Saturday night, when I picked up Fritz, the best friend I ever had. I lived in Orange County, and he lived in North Long Beach. I had to take the 91 to get to his house. The 91 was a busy freeway, but I steeled my nerves that night to pick him up. His house was only the first stop. Our destination that night was L.A. We went to Club KIIS (*"kiss"*), a dance club hosted by the radio station 102.7 KIIS FM every Saturday night. It was a long drive but I figured sooner or later I just had to get over myself and drive on the freeway. Clubbing became my favorite thing to do on the weekends. I wasn't a very good dancer, but I broke out of my shell and just started to learn how to move my body with the beat in an un-awkward way. I probably looked silly, but in the middle of a crowded dance floor I would dance well enough to not stick out.

Fritz and I frequented different clubs on the weekends. We

went to Club KIIS a few times, but because of the distance we eventually stopped going and decided to just go to the ones in Orange County. During one of the nights we went to Club KIIS, however, there was a certain TV personality who was carrying a clipboard. He was known as "*Larry the Loser.*" He was this crazy-haired guy from MTV. That night he was accepting sign-ups for a chance to be in an episode of "*Singled Out,*" an MTV dating show. Fritz and I signed up and were both invited to appear on the show. Naturally we accepted. Who wouldn't want to be on MTV? Mind you, I was not a Christian yet. It wouldn't be too much longer before I would get saved, but at the time I was still basically a *degenerate*. Of course I would welcome any opportunity to hang out with a bunch of girls in bikinis, especially when it meant taking part in one of the hottest MTV shows of the day.

When we arrived, the first thing the producers made everybody do was get rid of their pens. Singled Out was a TV show, *not a bar*. The producers had a show to film and a strict schedule to follow. They didn't want the boys hitting on the girls and trying to get phone numbers. Then, prior to filming, the guys lined up in front of judges to be assessed. One by one, the guys would stand in front of these judges to take their shirt off to be divided into two categories—"*ripped*" if they're impressively muscular or "*gypped*" if they were anything but. Fritz was "ripped" and I was designated "gypped." It was no surprise and I wasn't hurt or anything, it was part of the show. I knew about it and I actually stepped up my workouts to prepare for this event just to tone up enough to not be too embarrassing when I removed my shirt, even as a "gypped" guy. Dancing was a big part of the show. There's frequent dancing in the background. One of the things the producers told us to do was to dance with our arms in the air. It looked livelier on TV that way, they explained. I felt like I learned some insider secret. At any rate, I was just one of the extras who paraded in front of the selected bachelorette. I never even saw the episode I was in. But somebody somewhere did. It was my two seconds of fame. Today I can honestly brag that I was on MTV with Carmen Electra.

6. THE CONVERSION

I was raised as a Roman Catholic. I got saved when I was around 21 years of age. A lot of Christians can point to a specific date they got born again. I can't say exactly when it happened. It actually used to concern me that I couldn't pinpoint the year, let alone the very day I became a real Christian. It made me wonder whether or not I truly got saved. Everybody else I've talked to seemed to know precisely the moment when they got saved. My concern wasn't really serious because I knew that I was saved. I know that I *am* saved. My salvation doesn't rest upon my remembrance of the exact day it took place. No, it rests upon the promises of God as recorded in His Word. First John 5:13 says, *"These things I have written unto you who believe in the name of the Son of God, that you may know you have eternal life."*

I was raised by religious parents who did a fantastic job of instilling in me some strong morals. They are Roman Catholics and at the time of this writing, sadly, I cannot say that they've been born again. But when it came to doing the right things, they're pretty spot-on. If salvation was based on works and if God graded on a curve, I'd say they'd have a pretty good shot of making it through the pearly gates. But that's not what the Bible teaches. Ephesians 2:8-9 states, *"For by grace you have been saved through faith and that not of yourselves; it is the gift of God, not of works, lest anyone should boast."* I was a good boy growing up. I didn't get into trouble, didn't do drugs, didn't get any girl pregnant or join any gangs. I behaved like a Christian *outwardly*, probably even more so than a lot of real Christians. As a result, my testimony isn't nearly as spectacular as those who were involved in a bunch of worldly and immoral stuff. Those who used to party and break the law show a dramatic change in their outward behavior after becoming a Christian. But I was *already* well-behaved, and I *already* led a relatively moral life *prior* to getting saved. The

Bible says that anyone in Christ is a new creation. For me, most of the changes were *internal*.

There were four specific things that changed in my heart when I got saved. First, I developed a *hunger* for the Word of God. Nobody forced me to read the Bible. I wanted to do it. I took notes and typed up verses that jumped out at me. I bought supplementary material and learned some apologetics. Second, I wanted *to be with other believers*. I was eager to find a Christian church because for the first time in my life, I was able to worship the Lord in *freedom*. I wasn't going to do it to earn His favor or to try to make it to heaven; I wanted to do it out of a deep *gratitude* towards what He's done for me on the cross. Third, the world's value *dropped*. I didn't care for the material things nearly as much. I'm not talking about not wanting to buy cool stuff anymore, I still do. But I completely lost interest in trying to impress people and bringing glory to *myself*. The only thing I wanted to boast about was my *relationship with the Lord*. Fourth were my feelings towards my parents.

Right before I got saved, I had serious animosity towards them. I blamed my parents for everything wrong in my life and I saw them as my enemies. I'm not suggesting that I had no reason to feel the way I did. In fact, if I got into the details most would probably agree that my anger was justified. But when I got born again, God instantly removed that feeling and replaced it with *compassion*. I kid you not. It happened right away. It wasn't a process that I had to work on over a period of time. One day I just found myself not being mad at my parents anymore. For whatever wrong they may have done me, I forgave them in my heart. The change inside me was so dramatic that I was a little embarrassed about it. I did not want my parents to think I was weird or losing my mind. For a while I actually *pretended* to be angry with my parents and did my best to act the way I used to when I still hated them.

So how did I get saved? The real answer is that *the Holy Spirit spoke to me*. I started reading the Bible at first to reinforce my Roman Catholic faith. But the more I read, the more I realized that the teachings of the Catholic Church were *contradictory* to the Bible when it came to matters of salvation, among other things. At some point I knew I needed to make a decision. I could choose to accept the Bible as the final authority, or I could choose the teachings of the Catholic Church. I chose the Bible. One of the first verses that spoke to my heart was John 5:24. *"Most assuredly, I say to you, he who hears My word and believes in Him who sent Me has everlasting life, and shall not come into judgment, but has passed from death to life."* I remember crying out to the Lord after reading that, almost like a bratty child, saying to Him in my heart, *"These are YOUR words! I'm going to hold you to them!"* That *may* have been the moment I got saved. If not, it was a great starting point nonetheless.

The Lord guided me to learn the essentials of the faith through various Christian radio programs. Roughly a year earlier, at Cal State Long Beach, God even had some people from the Campus Crusade for Christ *illustrate* to me what Jesus did on the cross, which didn't have an effect on me until the appointed time of my salvation, at which point everything just made sense. I clearly remember standing in my living room and coming to the realization that the meaning of life is *Jesus*. I then started listening to evangelist Greg Laurie's radio program *"A New Beginning"* every morning as I drove to CSULB. During one of his programs he invited his listeners to accept Jesus Christ and pray along with him a simple prayer, which I did. A lot of Christians refer to it as *"The Sinner's Prayer,"* which is basically an admission that you've broken God's commandments and therefore deserve hell, then repenting, asking for God's forgiveness and putting your faith in Christ. It's not so much the words as it is what's taking place inside your heart. So I did that in the car as I was driving, but most likely it was just a formality at that point, my own personal ceremony *after the fact*.

That was over twenty years ago. My walk with the Lord is far from perfect, but His truth is something that I could never turn my back on because it would violate and defy *all* logic. It is literally impossible to denounce genuine faith in Christ. Once you've been born again, you can't be *un-born*. To deny the truth the Holy Spirit has revealed to you is like denying that a triangle has three sides or insisting that five plus five equals anything other than ten. Now a person who doesn't know anything about geometry or math could conceivably say these things in their ignorance, but once they've learned and understood, there's simply no going back. It's the same way with Christ.

7. BEER GOGGLES

*O*ne of the more interesting things in my becoming a Christian was the timing. There were definitely things going on in the spiritual realm. I got saved right around the time I was just getting into the world. By the world's standards I was kind of a late bloomer. Things that most people started getting into during high school, I only started to dabble with during my college years. I've told you how I was a goody-two-shoes before I became a Christian, which is true for the most part. But shortly before I was born again, I had definitely become less of a goody-two-shoes. I was more mature, for one thing, and my priorities had shifted from daydreaming about the perfect romance, to pursuing more readily available and tangible goals, if you catch my drift. Also, my mojo was beginning to kick in. I had shed a considerable amount of the awkwardness and self-doubt I bore throughout high school and had transformed into more or less a normal guy. And I began to reap the rewards thereof. It was all God's grace that I didn't descend into a life of total depravity.

Every salvation story is a miracle, regardless of the background. One of the miracles in mine is how I managed to find the time to think about the things of God while I was running amok in the world like a kid in a candy store. There were a lot of temptations that had all of a sudden gotten within my reach. Maybe it was the result of having a better fashion sense and cutting my big hair down to within acceptable social norms. In reality, however, it was all spiritual. I'm not the type to pretend I see what's going on behind the scenes and what the Lord is up to exactly. I'm actually quite peeved by people who try to explain the tough times they may be going through as some sort of test the Lord is putting them through prior to the wonderful blessings He has waiting for them. I don't like to sound like a pessimist, but the Bible only promises that everything will be made right once we make it into eternity, in the presence of the Lord. That's when all our trials and tribulations will end and our every tear wiped away. Not necessarily in this life. In fact, definitely not in this life, regardless of how great and drama-free our lives turn out to be. When we face trials, it's not our business to declare that God is only doing it to make us stronger or so that we can glorify Him through it all. Sometimes, crap just happens. It may or may not get resolved in our lifetimes. It may never ever make sense why God permitted whatever in our lives. I'm still a little upset that God made me so short. There are hundreds of thousands of people that are way over six feet tall. God could've shaved off an inch each from 5 extremely tall people and added it to my height. I would've been a million times happier and those tall guys wouldn't have even noticed. Stuff like that doesn't make sense. And then I think of actual midgets then I feel a little better. But that's beside the point.

My point is, not everything has a reason that will be revealed to us in this lifetime, and if you're one of those people who think they know the why to every what, then you are fooling yourself or you are full of it. My actual point is, however, that while I'm not that kind of Christian, I will say that the reason behind my improved social life was all spiritual. I was close to getting saved, and maybe things like this are clearly visible to the key players in the spiritual realm from both sides of the battle. The enemy was either throwing stuff at me to keep me away from God or to try to get me to do something that would ruin the rest of my earthly life even if I did get saved. When I got saved, the party didn't come to a full stop. It sorta went on for a little while, but God did put a spiritual leash on me. Like Paul talked about, there was now this war between my flesh and my spirit. There was restraint on my actions and wisdom in my decisions. I knew when to say when, and when I didn't, God Himself would put a lid on it.

One incident in which I did know when to say when took place at a club in Whittier. I was with my best friend Fritz and we were looking pretty sharp that night. We were on the floor busting our moves without any dance partners, which isn't *that* weird. The typical dance floor would consist of a few couples, small groups of girls dancing amongst themselves and some scattered lone wolves who are hoping that someone would dance with them. That would be me and Fritz. On this night, one of the few of times that a girl actually danced with me in a club, one came up to me and was a little more passionate than the typical girl who just wanted to get her groove on. First, she stopped right in front of me and just *stared* for a few seconds. She then put her hand on my chest and started rubbing it before putting her arms around my neck and started dancing. I put my arms around her waist and we danced for a little while. It was obvious to me that she was *under the influence*. If I didn't know any better I'd say that she was under *my* spell. But as handsome as I'd like to believe I was that night, I knew I didn't look *that* hot. Nope, them's definitely beer goggles she's got on. She then moved her face real close to mine and tried to kiss me. I turned my head at the last moment but kept on dancing. I gave her a little friendly smile. She then made another attempt at my mouth but she was no match for my cat-like (*and alcohol-free*) reflexes and I dodged her again perfectly. During this whole time her girlfriends were standing nearby giggling, finding the whole thing amusing. I looked at them and smiled as their friend and I continued to dance with each other. I could tell that they appreciated the fact that I wasn't taking advantage of her. They eventually would pry her off of me. I looked at Fritz and we both shrugged our shoulders. That was a fun night. I'm very thankful for the power God gave me that night to not be anything less than a gentleman.

8. FIGHT CLUB

*I*f I became a professional boxer, I would not be the most exciting fighter to watch. I wouldn't have been boring, but I definitely wouldn't have been the buzzsaw Manny Pacquiao was in his prime. I would not be running around like a wuss, but I think I'm a natural counterpuncher. I really like to observe things and assess the battlefield before making a move. I guess I would've been what boxing fans like to call a "safety first" type of fighter. Kind of like Floyd Mayweather Jr., I suppose. My number one priority would've been to ensure I took as little damage as possible.

I've never been in a fist fight and I probably never will. No, I *never* will, period. There's just no scenario I could think of that could lure me into trading punches with anybody. It's just not worth it. The only thing remotely possible would be if some random punk in public started swinging at me either to impress his friends or because he was a *racist*. If that ever happened I would be forced to defend myself. I don't ever plan to just stand there and get beat up. My plan is to put my guard up, use some fancy footwork and block and parry as many of the guy's punches until he realizes what he's up against, stops throwing punches, says a parting phrase filled with cuss words and walks away pretending he got the better of me. As you can see, my plan doesn't involve me throwing any punches. Punching back would be my *last* resort. If it ever got to that point, I would rely on a couple of stiff left jabs to put an end to the altercation. My bare fists landing on the bridge of the guy's nose ought to have enough force to break it or at least bloody it. If I land on his eye socket it could instantly swell shut. By then I hope the guy would have the sense to realize it's not going to end well for him and just give up. Or, it could *escalate* and turn into a knockdown, drag out affair, in which case I would count it as a loss on my part. I would literally just tell the guy that he had won and ask him to just stop. Hopefully by then security would've arrived to break it up. Hopefully.

Notice that I don't ever picture myself actually losing these encounters. It doesn't mean it's not possible. Heck it's probably *probable*. This is why I go to great lengths to not ever end up in a situation where I'd be forced to fight. It's become a lesser concern over the years as I had gotten older and left the scene made for the younger guys. I no longer go to places where it's possible to look at somebody the *wrong way* or hit on somebody's girl. I don't have to prove anything to anybody anymore and I'm mostly at peace with who I am. I'm not looking for opportunities to show how *macho* I could be. Nope, I'm a safety first type of guy, and pretty much *always* have been.

I recall this one specific night Fritz and I were at a club just dancing the night away hoping to meet some females. Well *that* didn't happen, but fists did start flying somewhere. I don't know if it happened on the dance floor or closer to the bar area. To be honest I didn't even see any fight. All I know was that there was this big commotion and that it *felt* like there was a brawl, or that one was brewing. My survival instincts kicked in and I was at the exit in two seconds *flat*. Fritz would tell me later that he saw the fight break out and wanted to point it out to me, but that when he turned his head towards me he saw that I was practically out the door already. That's who I am. *Safety first.* I didn't care to stick around for what could've been an all-out melee. Somebody could've pulled a knife or a gun, threw chairs or broke bottles over someone's head. You know, kind of like the Wild West. Luckily whatever it was got shut down pretty quickly by the bouncers. I was proud of my escape. I was also glad that I got to go back in and dance some more.

9. I REALLY (DON'T) WANT TO KISS YOU

When I was still in the game, you could say that I did-n't have the best of luck with women. The first three official girlfriends I had all cheated on me. There were a few I dated but were never officially my girlfriends. Those lost interest quickly and bailed out on me. I viewed myself as a hopeless romantic during the prime of my young adulthood. I was always looking for the right woman to fall in love with, although I had no idea what kind of qualities I should be look-ing for in the right woman. I was very naïve in my twenties. I was also pretty clingy, which contributed to my getting cheat-ed on and dumped.

I never understood the logic behind that. Personally, I think clingy is a good trait to have. I want to be with someone who needs me and will not trade me for the world. I'm not a huge fan of "giving each other space." I mean, I'd give space if the other person asks for it, but I never need it for myself. I don't find fault with people who require a certain amount of space. I accept that people are different and that the Lord made us all to be unique with different personalities and thought patterns and stuff. It doesn't mean that I understand people who need space. I don't think I ever will. It just makes zero sense to me. Why would you want to be apart from those that supposedly mean so much to you? How do people you supposedly love become something you'd want to keep away from, even for a brief moment? How can one see it a blessing to be temporarily separated from those they claim to care about the most? How can one go from *"I want to be with you forever,"* to *"I need to be alone for a little while,"* and then back to *"I want to be with you forever, again?"* To me that sounds like a *mental illness*.

If you pay attention to the lyrics of the greatest love songs from different eras, you'll notice a common theme—*together forever, together wherever*. It's okay to sing about it, but when a guy like me comes along who happens to be *the real deal*, he's considered *clingy*. Whatever. If I'm being honest with myself, there are a lot more undesirable things about me besides being needy. To be perfectly blunt, I'm simply not what many would consider a *keeper*. I'm not throwing a pity party or anything. I believe that I *am* very much a keeper. I *know* that I am a keeper. That is a fact and is not even in question. However it doesn't mean that the rest of the world sees it that way. Most don't, but that's okay, I don't need more than one girl to see me as a prize. I don't need the entire female population to see me as God's gift to women. I just need *one* woman to see that I'm God's gift to *her*. That woman is now my wife.

However, I do know one particular girl who definitely thought that I was *not* a gift to her or *any* woman, for that matter. I was kind of a jerk to her. I met her over the internet and we chatted a few times. We agreed to meet in person one day. I sent her my picture but she didn't have any, so I only went by her description, which sounded alright to me. You have to understand, this took place before anybody had smartphones and when almost everyone's internet used a dial-up connection (I still miss that modem noise). We agreed to meet somewhere neutral, I don't remember exactly where. But when we both stepped out of our cars, she turned out to be not quite as I had imagined. She was very unattractive, to put it mildly. Her face looked like a man's face. She wasn't actually a guy, just to clarify, but she really did have manly facial features. Okay, maybe she didn't. I'm just having a hard time saying straight up that she was *butt-ugly*. There, I said it. Go on, judge me, I don't care. I was actually repulsed. To her credit, she did warn me ahead of time that she was ugly. I made the mistake of giving her the benefit of the doubt. In my mind she was just battling with insecurity as some girls (and guys) do, but would turn out to be cute. But nope, this one was very *honest*. We didn't really have a plan to do anything or go anywhere, so I thought up an excuse on the spot to get away as quickly as possible. I told her that I had to go to a *funeral*. Mind you I was wearing blue jeans and a shiny blue shirt with some abstract swirly things on it, totally un-funeral-like. But going to a funeral was the only excuse I could think of that I felt comfortable ditching her for. She said that she'd like to go with me anyway, but I told her that would not be a good idea. I took my lies a step further. It was stupid and lame, but I said, *"Man I really wanna kiss you!"* I said it kind of in a way to suggest that *if* I had it my way that evening, I would *totally* want to kiss her, but since I *didn't* have it my way because you know, *funeral*, then I was just going to have to miss out on that privilege. I was so lucky that she didn't take me up on that kiss right there and then. So she bought it, or maybe she didn't. She probably saw right through my lies and realized that she failed to meet my expectations. It was the last time I ever saw her and that was the end of it. We may have said hi to each other online a couple of times after, but that was it.

Yes, I was a jerk, I fully admit it. Yes, I was being superficial. But it would've been much worse to lead her on and get her hopes up for *nothing*. At least that's what I kept telling myself to help me sleep better at night for the next several nights. I felt bad. For real. The truth is, I probably could've taken her to the movies or maybe to some nearby diner just to be friendly, but I didn't want to be seen in public with her, especially by someone I knew. Yes, that was pretty evil on my part. I am ashamed of what I did. I'm pretty sure I was already a Christian at the time, so the conviction was worse. Otherwise, I could've laughed it off and moved on with no problem. I was already a follower of Christ when I got into the three relationships I mentioned. They did me wrong and scarred me for the *rest of my life*. I always think that I was the victim, and perhaps I was. But I think I totally deserved it. It wasn't just this one girl. There were others that I knew better than to lead on, but did anyway, ignoring the Holy Spirit's direction. If I were to guess, I'd say that the bad relationships I had were a form of chastisement from the Lord. Yes, I know that I mentioned in an earlier story that I'm not one of those people who like to put meaning behind every setback in their lives. I'm making an exception for these. I still won't say it with 100% certainty, but I think it's a safe bet that God was chastising me, for the Bible says that *"for whom the Lord loves He chastens, and scourges every son whom He receives."* I'm perfectly fine with that.

10. 105 MY "A"

*F*rom the mid to late 90s, I had my fair share of internet meet ups with females, all in the name of *love*. I could probably write an entire book about it, but I would probably overdose on cringe if I had to recall every little detail. In those days I think it was a little more exciting due to the technological limitations that we didn't realize were technological limitations. The distinct, almost otherworldly sound the modem makes while it's trying to connect to the internet is the sound of *possibilities*. It's almost as though you're going through a portal not knowing what's on the *other side*. The fact that not too many people had access to a scanner meant that you'd have to take each other's word for it when it came to describing your appearance. If you're too young to remember what a scanner is for, it's used to scan actual physical photographs to transfer to your computer, where you can send it to others via email. Without a picture, however, it felt like scratching off a lottery ticket. Upon reading someone's physical specifications like height, weight and their hair color, your imagination goes on overdrive as it runs through all the possible permutations. There's magic in that. You never know what you're going to get when you finally meet the person. And *that* was exciting.

Some of the girls I talked to online would say they mildly resembled a particular actress, or so their friends told them. You knew that they couldn't *possibly* look like anyone famous or else they wouldn't be trying to meet guys over the internet, but then again you're sort of doing the exact same thing so you give them the *benefit* of the doubt. It's a game with complicated rules, or as Captain Barbossa might put it, more like *guidelines*. You want to be as honest as possible without selling yourself short. Speaking of which, I am short, so that's one of the things I hated talking about. I found that the revelation of my height has the power to end instant messages *instantly.* The internet is not the friendliest of places and you must learn to thicken your skin and just move on.

Now here's a confession I have to make. I'm not particularly attracted to *large* women. I know it sounds superficial. But on the flip side, not too many women are attracted to short guys, and I don't hold that against them. I'm not going to judge; we are *all* entitled to our own preferences. At least fat women can *diet.* I, on the other hand, have no hope. One thing I learned very early on was that women are not very honest when it comes to revealing their weight over the internet. Even the legit skinny ones would subtract 10 pounds from their real weight. The real fat ones would *divide* by two. Or three. So you wise up and look for the telltale signs. *"A real lady never reveals her weight,"* is a good one. Or, *"I don't like to give out my weight because muscle weighs more than fat."* Rrright. Some are a little more honest and say that they have *"a few extra pounds,"* which more accurately translates to *"a boatload of extra pounds."* But there are some who are actually honest. They describe themselves as a "BBW," which I believe stands for *"big burly woman."* I don't think it's the most flattering of terminologies, but more power to them. I learned that most fat girls get really creative when describing their bodies and would resolve to euphemisms like *"curvy,"* which really means *"lumpy,"* or *"well-endowed,"* when the rest of them is just as big as their chest.

I don't mean to go off on fat chicks; I'm just saying that God made people in all shapes and sizes. Just be *honest.* There are *lots* of guys out there who love bigger women. Much more than there are women who like *short guys.* I *never* lied about my height. You know why? Because when I finally meet the girl in person she'll see that I'm short. It's simple logic. Somehow, a lot of women don't think we're going to notice *"the few extra pounds"* they forgot to mention. So anyway, after a ton (pun totally intended) of experience, I discovered a near foolproof way of determining a girl's physique. I would ask every girl I talked to online if they wore *bangs.* Most women don't feel threatened by questions pertaining to their hairstyle and they answer truthfully when I ask them whether or not they have bangs. Why such an odd question? Well as it turns out, from the data I gathered, *around 80%* of girls who wore bangs during that time period were *fat.* Maybe it was just a coincidence, but it was pretty reliable. I proudly call this my *"Big Bang Theory."*

It wasn't a perfect system, but whenever a girl told me that she wore bangs, I would stop my pursuit right there and then.

So at any rate, there was this one girl I talked to online who wanted to meet up with me. She was going to take her best friend along and so I took my best friend Fritz with me, for a double blind date. The girl told me on more than a few occasions that she weighed 105 pounds. *Petite*. Then the night before we met in person, she told me she was so happy because she weighed herself that morning and she dropped down to *102 pounds*. I was thinking great; at least weight won't be an issue with her. So the evening of our meeting came, and Fritz and I were driving around the parking lot looking for her car, and we spotted her and her friend. I had a clear view of her face and it was obvious that she had flat out lied about her weight. The first words that came out of my mouth were, *"105 my a**!"* I proceeded to repeat those words several times while Fritz laughed his head off. Maybe the scale was broken. Or maybe she really meant *kilos*. We still went on with the double date. We walked around Huntington Beach for a couple of hours or so. Hopefully that started her off on her road to skinniness. And that was that. And yes, she wore bangs. I will forever be grateful for her priceless contribution to my Big Bang Theory.

11. MIRACLE JOB

I believe that the Word of God is sufficient for revealing Himself to us. He doesn't need to peek through the clouds to give us a glimpse of His face. He doesn't need to speak to us *audibly* by means of a burning bush. He doesn't need to give us *stuff*. He doesn't need to spare us from trials. As the Lord said to Paul after he had asked Him to remove the thorn in his side, His grace is sufficient indeed. The just shall live by faith, the Bible says. I've been a Christian for over 20 years and while I've grown in wisdom and understanding and have gotten to know the Lord better, I can't honestly say that my faith is stronger than when I first believed. I'm not talking about matters of salvation or my Christian faith in general. I'm not at all suggesting that I'm having doubts about the teachings of the Bible. It has nothing to do with that. I'm talking about faith in the sense of God simply *being there for me*, for my *practical* needs, and sometimes even my *impractical* ones.

I always like to say that while I know the Lord loves me in a theological sense, I'm not so sure that He actually *likes* me. I know it's borderline blasphemous for me to think that way, but sometimes I really do feel as though God doesn't care for me personally, and that while He sent His son to die on the cross, He did it for everybody else's sins and not particularly for my sins, and I just so happen to be covered as part of the clause. Now I know this couldn't be further from the truth. The Bible instructs us to cast our cares upon Jesus for He cares about us. *He cares about me*. It doesn't matter how I feel, His word trumps my emotions. I know this and yet I let my feelings get the better of me more often than I care to admit. I think that this happens to a lot of Christians. In part our flesh is to blame. As long as we're in this world we will be at war with our own flesh as our spirit aims to please the Lord. Satan also has a role to play in all this. That's what he does. He casts *doubt*. He'll lead you away from the Lord and then be the first one to accuse you should you stumble even in the slightest. I still struggle with doubt, but I am really thankful for having a solid Biblical foundation. I've been blessed to have attended churches that faithfully teach the Word of God when I was a young believer. Sadly, I can't confidently say the same about every believer. I know way too many Christians who are content to partake only of milk and do not care to move on to solid food, as Hebrews 5 puts it. They make themselves easy pickings for false doctrines and deceptions. I'm not immune to being deceived, but I'm at least aware enough to realize when I'm being deceived, whether I'm deceiving *myself* or being deceived by outside forces. By God's grace I have enough wisdom to see it when it's happening and be able to make a conscious decision to step out of that deception. Still, I'm of little faith.

A lot of times I don't believe God cares about my day to day problems. He's got me covered for eternity, that's great and wonderful. What about this life? I know that life is but a vapor, but it could certainly seem like an eternity especially during the rough times. The thing of it is that the Bible clearly states that God *demonstrates* His love for us in that while we were yet sinners, He died for us. The Bible doesn't say that the Lord demonstrates His love for us by giving us an easy life, healing our ailments, hooking us up with that dream job or *making us taller* (I had to throw that one in there!). He doesn't need to do any of that to prove His love for us. He proved it by dying on the cross for our sins. A lot of Christians, myself included, profess this with a lot of passion and reverence because Jesus dying on the cross for us is kind of a big deal. The truth of it is that we really have no idea just *how* big a deal it truly was. We don't know how it all worked in the spiritual realm and we don't know how the transaction was conducted or exactly how Jesus' righteousness was *imputed* to us. I have no clue. All I know is that it is true and I can take it all the way to the bank. God *demonstrates* His love by dying on the cross for us lousy sinners, this much is clear. What the Bible does *not* say is that the *only way* God demonstrates His love for us is by dying on the cross. *Nothing* says that God *can't* show His love for us in other ways.

I believe that God grants every believer what I like to call,

"God moments." That is, specific situations where you know beyond any doubt, that God was directly involved. One such moment I had happened not too long after I got saved. My dad, who was in his early 50s at the time, suffered a mild stroke. And by mild, I mean couldn't have been any milder. He didn't fall over or anything like that. He sorta just started acting weird, like half asleep, speaking utter nonsense. I'll never forget that day. He went to work and came back early in the day. He walked through the front door but there was a guy behind him. It was a co-worker that I had never met. My dad walked in and offered him something to drink. But this dude had the grimmest expression on his face. He looked at me and said, *"You need to take him to the doctor right now."* Why he didn't just take my dad to the doctor instead of our house I couldn't' tell you, but apparently my dad was having lunch at a restaurant and he just dropped his fork and couldn't pick it up though he kept on trying. That's when everyone noticed something was wrong. By the grace of God my dad didn't keel over and was good enough to walk on his own two feet, although his mind was in *la-la land*. I drove him to the doctor, who determined that my dad had a mild stroke. He was hospitalized for a couple of nights. I remember him being admitted on a Wednesday night and being released the following Friday afternoon.

When my dad was still at the hospital and my mom was at home stressing out I reassured her that God *will* take care of this. What happened that Friday morning was one of my first God moments. I received a phone call out of nowhere, from a temp agency. They offered me a full time job literally out of the blue, to start working on *Monday*. It was my very first job *ever*. I was not looking for a job at the time but when I got that call, I knew for certain it was from God. It turned out that my dad wasn't permitted to go back to work for a few weeks, and I became the only source of income for our family. Now I made but a fraction of what my dad did, but it was enough to at least slow down the bleeding until my dad was able to work again. What happened was that a few months earlier, perhaps even a year prior, I had turned in an application to the company my aunt worked at. I don't even remember what I had applied for and the funnier thing was that I have no clue how my application ended up at a temp agency when I had turned it in directly to the company through my aunt. Maybe that was one of the ways they hired people, I don't know. But the *timing* of it all made it clear that it was *unmistakably* God looking out for my *practical* needs. I could've gotten that job several months earlier, but God made sure it happened on the very day I needed it the most. There wasn't even an interview or anything. The agency just told me that I could start working on Monday. That was it. That was the Lord.

12. FULLERTON

Nothing helps you get over a breakup like meeting a new prospect. I guess it all depends on the type of relationship you were in. Sometimes, even bad breakups can be *oh so good*. The immediate freedom that follows an abusive relationship is like the instant relief one gets from *puking* after being carsick for hours. Not all breakups have to be nasty, though. On rare occasions, the dumper could be pretty nice to the *dumpee*. I got dumped by this really pretty girl who was really nice. Her name was Diana. I almost wouldn't count it as getting dumped because we were "together" for literally a week before she wised up and realized what a loser I was. As ugly as I am, I could be quite charming under the right circumstances. I do have my moments. I managed to woo Diana into dating me and I guess we both sorta agreed at some point that we were *official*. But let's face it, unless you're in elementary school, going out with someone for a week is *nothing*. So in my book we were *not* official, hence the breakup doesn't really count as one. If it were a marriage, it wouldn't have been a divorce but an annulment. Same difference, right? Whatever. The brevity of it didn't really help me feel better at the time. The girl was nice and cute in so many ways. Diana was the perfect *girlfriend material*, someone who'll make you feel good and you'd want to drag around wherever you went because your stock went up when you're together. But that wasn't why I wanted to be with her, I don't care about any of that popularity stuff, I wasn't trying to look cool. I just wanted to be happy and I was in it for the long haul.

I'm *always* in it for the long haul. I never go into a relationship unless I'm willing to go the distance. The way I see it, you never really know who the right one is. I don't want to end up treating the right one the *wrong* way because I was too dense to realize she was *the one*. The only way I could avoid doing that is to treat *every* girl as though she was the *one*, even if she ends up being the *worst*. I'd rather see a guilty suspect go free than for an innocent one to get the electric chair. There's a price to pay to live by this philosophy. I had to be willing to put *myself* in the position to get *hurt*. In fact, this kind of mentality *requires* that I be the one who gets hurt. I'd rather be wronged than be the one doing the wronging. It's much easier to live with yourself this way. Diana didn't really do anything wrong, though. She just realized she didn't like me as much as she thought she did, and moved on. She was nice about it, but it still *stung*. I was in my early 20s so I had my whole life ahead of me and I wouldn't even call it a setback. It was still *party time*, no need to settle down.

So what did I do? A couple of nights after I got dumped, I drove around town with my best friend Fritz, of course. I also took my cousin Jerry who was a little younger than me. At the time he was kind of the timid one, so I thought it'd do him good to see how a *real man* like me went out to meet girls. I was *feeling it* that night. Sometimes you just have those nights where everything is clicking and you feel like you can take on the world. That night I hit a *homer*. Well, it's a homerun *for me*. Most guys would probably have considered it a *foul ball* at best. But for a guy with my batting average, the ball making any type of contact with the bat would be the equivalent of a *grand slam*. So we were driving through the city of Fullerton and as luck would have it, we hit a red light right next to a carful of pretty girls. I didn't hesitate. I instinctively rolled down my window and asked the girl closest to me if she knew which way it was to Fullerton. Now I knew exactly where we were, and I knew that I couldn't have said anything *dumber*. What I didn't know was that it was actually going to lead to something positive. She responded with, *"Is that the best line you can come up with?"* A boyish grin formed across my face as I answered, *"I don't know, maybe?"* The other girls in the car were giggling which I thought was a good sign, so I went for it. *"Do you wanna pull over?"* To my surprise she actually agreed. We turned at the very next street and pulled over to the sidewalk. Everybody got out of their cars and we introduced ourselves to each other. During that moment though, it was all about me and that girl. She gave me her phone number and before I went back into my car, I took her hand and kissed it, to her delight and her friends' amusement. They were like,

"Whoa, there!"

It was a successful evening of joyriding for a loser like me. My best friend was kind of amazed as was my cousin. The way it went down was almost like a scene ripped straight out of *Fast and Furious*, if you took down the cool factor a notch or two. It wasn't the only time I pulled off something *suave* like that (suave for me, anyway), but it was one of the best ones. I believe I called the girl a few days later and we talked on the phone briefly, but that was it. We never met up or anything. I don't remember what happened exactly. But I do know that it helped me out tremendously in getting over my *disappointment* (I wouldn't really call it a heartbreak) with Diana. On that night in Fullerton, California, on Commonwealth Avenue, *I hit it out of the park.*

13. REDEMPTION

Remember "Berklee in L.A.?" You know, the band camp I went to. Well, I got the chance do it again two years later. I would've gone every year if I could, but taking a year off did me a lot of good. A lot of things happened in two years. I had gotten a full time job and still had the same job when I went to Berklee in L.A. I was still fairly new at my job but my superiors let me have some time off even though technically I hadn't earned my vacation days just yet, because I was such an outstanding employee, according to them. I also started taking sax lessons from a world renowned saxophonist, which caused my sax skills to spike. I had a massive *musical* growth spurt. So when I set foot once more on the campus of Claremont McKenna College, I had confidence like I never had before. I may not have been the best sax player there, but I knew that I could hang with *any* musician. There were some returning students that I recognized and was cool with instantly, and thankfully that weirdo older sax player didn't come back, or else I may have gotten myself into trouble once more.

The first good sign of things to come happened within the first 15 minutes of my arrival. I was in line to get registered and checked in, and there was this pretty hot chick right behind me. I struck up a casual conversation and we hit it off. Her name was Brandy and she played flute. After we got done with the registration, we walked off together and were nearly inseparable for the next three days. We'd only split up whenever we went to our respective classes. We became pretty close in such a short amount of time. We didn't exactly fall in love, but we grew *really, really* fond of each other. We made out *a lot*. Our feelings for each other hit its peak on the third night, I believe. Earlier in the day Brandy had talked about having issues with her assigned roommate and how she couldn't stand her. That evening I got a knock on my door. It was Brandy. There she was standing on the doorstep with her luggage. She wanted to move in. For whatever reason, my assigned roommate was a no show so I had the dorm to myself. I let her in and told her she could stay.

I've gone through quite the transformation since high school, where I was 0 for 100 with girls. Then there I was, with some gorgeous girl I barely knew, showing up at my doorstep asking me if she could spend the night. But something else happened to me since my last outing at Berklee in L.A; I got *born again*. I was a genuine Christian when Brandy spent the night with me. It was an emotional night filled with *passion*. But not only did I *not* cross the line, I barely flinched as I looked temptation in the eye. Brandy and I kissed as much as we talked that night. But that was *all*, and it was all because of God. Brandy took the initiative by showing up and asking to spend the night with me. She could've very easily taken it a step further by trying to seduce me. She never did. It didn't cross my mind to try to seduce her, either. I liked her a lot and I was content to play *tonsil hockey* all night. It was God's grace. It's the only logical explanation for my restraint. *Everything* was in place. It was mine for the taking. Now I know for sure it was the Lord because right after band camp, when I was in the flesh, I was kicking myself for not taking advantage of the opportunity. It turned out that Brandy was psycho. After that night she became standoffish and started acting strangely towards me. She moved back into her own dorm room the following day and wanted nothing to do with me. The rest of my stay felt super weird.

But it didn't matter; I was kicking butt with my *sax playing*. I was one of the best saxophonists in camp among the students. It was hands down *the* most gratifying musical experience of my *life*. There were jam sessions in the evening just like the last time I was there, but the difference this time was that I was getting down and grooving with my sax like I never have before. It was *amazing*. When it came time for the concert we were preparing for all week, I sounded like a pro during my solo. And yes, I had a solo this time. I had a different band director and there was no buffoon sax player that made me want to prank him. However, the band director who denied me my solo from two years prior was there again. He actually watched my performance. Afterwards I sat down with the audience, somewhere in the back row, to watch the other bands perform. That band director then sat at the very edge of my row, about 6 seats away from me. A couple of minutes later, he started scooting closer and closer to me until he reached the seat right next to mine. He then looked at me, shook my hand, congratulated me and told me I did a great job. He then got back up and walked away. That felt real good. I felt *redeemed*. He basically acknowledged my skills and my improvement since the last time he saw me, two years earlier. It was as though I had *earned* his respect, which was a big deal to me because I had a lot of respect for him and I really did feel like a *jackass* for doing what I did before. On the last day of camp when everyone was saying goodbye, one of the other saxophonists and his parents complimented me. He was a few years younger than me but he was pretty good. He asked me how old I was and I said, "*Twenty two.*" His exact response was, "*You're 22? No wonder you're so freaking good!*" And *that* was the icing on the cake.

14. THE LORD TAKETH AWAY

I've said it before and I'll say it again. I love making people laugh. It all stems from my *love* for humans, deep down inside. Not too many people would think that I'm a very social guy because I'm not outgoing. I'm *socially awkward*. I simply don't have much in common with most people. And I absolutely abhor small talk. It's like pulling teeth. Whenever I'm at any sort of gathering my goal is to just get through it unnoticed. My default strategy is to simply blend in and not attract any attention. I can't just sit still and be quiet, even though that's what I'd usually prefer to, because that's cue for some annoying extrovert to start chatting it up with me because it's his *sacred* duty to do so. I am very shy even though I've learned to mask that shyness over the years. I really do enjoy sitting and observing other people interact. Their lives are usually much more interesting than mine, and it just amuses me how I can continue to enjoy life despite having such an uneventful existence.

When I listen to people socialize at parties, I hear them talk about going on family vacations, going fishing, going hiking, going sailing, going up in the mountains and other stuff that begin with "*going*." Me, I "go" and play video games. My greatest adventures take place inside a TV screen. What I don't ever hear people talk about is what video games they're currently obsessed with or what game they most recently beat. They don't talk about any upcoming games and which ones they might be looking forward to the most. You'd think that with the video game industry being as big as it has gotten over the past two decades, you'd run into more gamers. That hasn't been the case with me. From my experience, most people see video games as a complete waste of time and tend to look down on those who play them. Most people I know act like video games are *beneath* them. I especially want to wring the necks of those who notice some minor oddity like an object clipping through a wall, make a comment on how silly it is and act like those are the very things that keep sophisticated people *like them* from getting into video games, because great humans *like them* won't settle for anything less than absolute perfection, and that one day, when video games are totally flawless in every imaginable way, then *maybe* they would consider playing. To those people I only have *two words* to say but since I'm writing this book to be read by people of all ages, I will refrain from putting those words down in writing.

As I've said before, I firmly believe that most people take themselves way too seriously, often to the point of *self-worship*, Christians included. It's become somewhat of a secondary mission of mine (*primary being to preach the Gospel whenever I recognize an opportunity*) to knock people off their high horses, not just for the sake of it, but so they can realize what a disgusting and stinky horse they've been sitting on this whole time. Then maybe they'd discover how much better it is to walk on the ground or else find a much shorter horse like those miniature ones you see in parades. *This* is why I love to pull pranks on people. I just want them to be able to laugh at themselves and see that we're *all* the same. In the grand scheme of things it doesn't matter if we're rich, poor, pretty, ugly, tall, short, skinny or fat; we were *all* created in God's image and have only *one* life to make a decision on Jesus. Sadly, most will *not* choose the Lord and will end up in the "smoking section" of eternity. The least I could do for them is to make them laugh in this life because where they're most likely going, there would only be *weeping and gnashing of teeth*.

The first job I ever had, that one miracle job I told you about, was a menial customer service position. I took orders over the phone for mail-in prescription drugs. I was really grateful for that job but it wasn't like a dream job or anything. I mean, seriously, how many kids ever dream of one day being tethered to their desk via headsets while getting yelled at by angry people? If I had to guess I'd say literally *zero*. Still, I had fun at that job and I was able to *share the Gospel* with at least one guy. I was also the funny guy who loved to mess around. I was shy, I *am* a shy, but once I've warmed up to people and gotten comfortable with them, I can be myself and be as goofy as I want. Not everybody appreciates my humor because it takes genius levels of intellect to get it, but geniuses do exist, you know?

One of my responsibilities as a customer service rep was to add new customers to our database. It's just basic data entry involving general information like names, phone numbers and addresses. As soon as the customer has been added to the database, the system would generate an account number for that customer. One day I had this brilliant idea to add fictitious names that sounded stupid, like "*Harry Ball*" or "*George Bushy*," for example. There were many others that were just absurd and not even the least bit clever. I would then call up my co-workers and have them type the account numbers and they would see the ridiculous names pop up. I did this for days, maybe *weeks*. They all got a good laugh out of them. It was a harmless thing as the accounts I created were "hollow." They didn't affect any of the existing customers' accounts. Unfortunately my mangers didn't see it that way. One day I got called into their office to verify that I was in fact the guy responsible for entering all those names into the system. Then I got *fired* on the spot. It was one of the most humiliating days of my life. There were two others in the room with me. One was a supervisor and one was the actual manager. As is the procedure with most companies, I had to be escorted out of the building. The manager was somewhat sympathetic, reminding me that I was still very young and that I can learn from this. As the supervisor was getting ready to walk me out through the office, the manager read the devastation in my face and told the supervisor that he'd walk me out himself. The manager took the back route rather than have me walk past my co-workers in shame.

That was the end of the miracle job God provided for me. The Lord taketh away. Ironically it happened on a Friday, the same day of the week I was offered the position. I lied to my parents when I got home, telling them that I quit my job. To make things more believable, I told them that I was to return on Monday for my exit interview, when in fact it was just to pick up my final check.

15. THE SIGNAL

I'm a passive-aggressive guy. In fact, I'm pretty sure I'm the very *personification* of it. This isn't more evident than when I post stuff on Facebook that are aimed towards very specific people on my friends list, but done in such a way as to not be 100% traceable to the people I intended it for. I don't like direct confrontation. There are few topics I will not hesitate to engage anybody on, like the Gospel and the infallibility of God's word, or how PC gaming will forever and ever suck, but with everything else I prefer to just *troll* people indirectly. When I troll people it's either because I don't care much for the subject or I feel that the person is hopeless and it's just fun to troll them (*yes, that's my flesh, sorry*). Usually it's due to the latter, particularly when I'm posting about politics.

I've never been into politics, but the Lord has instructed His children to be the light and salt of the world. There's never been a time in modern history in which Christians' participation in politics has been more critical than it is today. It's actually quite amazing how bold *evil* has become over the past decade. Believers know how it all comes down in the end and that ultimately, Jesus Himself will once and for all put an end to *all* evil. In the grand scheme of things, there's *nothing* anybody can do to bring peace to this world. As Christians, our hope is in the Lord, not in any politician. However that does *not* excuse us from not proclaiming the truth and fighting for what is right. We are light by *illuminating* the world and *exposing* its evils while making the truth known. We are salt by *preserving* what little good that's left in the world. We accomplish this through the ballots, conversations with people the Lord puts in our paths, and boldly *speaking out* against the rampant evils in today's society. I don't think God has given us the responsibility to *win* it, but He did order us to *fight* for what is right *in His eyes*.

A lot of people on my friend's list are not born again. It

baffles me how deceived they are. The truth is so obvious and the wicked are so easy to detect. Their deception is *spiritual*. It's the only logical explanation to their being so *oblivious*. I have to admit, they annoy the heck out of me because of how stupid they are, but I know that it really has nothing to do with their intelligence. Still, they're so arrogantly wicked, or wickedly arrogant, that I've basically dusted off my proverbial sandals. The only thing left for me to do on Facebook is to *troll* them. Share a post here, a meme there or type some impossibly *vague* remark. *Passive aggressive*.

I'm not one to get in direct confrontations because it's simply not who I am. But at the same time, my flesh is full of pride and I don't back down easily if I feel that I'm in the right and sometimes, even when I'm in the *wrong*. One such incident took place over twenty years ago as I was driving around in my neighborhood with my girlfriend, Anna (*who was the girlfriend from hell, but more on that later*). At the time I was still living with my parents in a *gated* community. Now the people who lived in this community were really caught up in the whole prestige thing. There was a homeowner's association that basically had the power to tell everybody within the gates what to do. If you allowed your grass to get an inch too tall, you're gonna hear it from the association. If you happened to be a non-conformist, you'll quickly get ostracized by the community and they can make your stay *miserable*. They're not someone you'd want to mess with, that's for sure. So there we were driving around and I had this 32-oz cup of soda. After we drove through the automatic gates, I stopped the car, opened my door and put the soda down on the ground. I was *littering*. I don't know why I did what I did, I honestly couldn't tell you. But it was just my luck that there was somebody driving right behind me, a homeowner's association *loyalist*. Now this guy wasn't passive aggressive. He was full on *confrontational*. He stopped just short of physically threatening me but he said in no uncertain terms that it would be in my best interest to not leave my trash there. I was kind of intimidated by this guy's ugly mug. He's the type who hates life because of how ugly he is, but rather than getting depressed about it, prefers to take it out on others. This guy was ugly and had *nothing* to lose. He most likely lowered the pitch of his voice to sound even *meaner*. I should've just picked up my cup and drove away. But I wasn't about to let this ugly dude whose parents were not married, tell me what to do, especially in front of my hot girlfriend. I wasn't about to cuss him out, either. Like I said, this guy had nothing to lose and as big a loser as I was, I had more to lose than he did. Rather than putting my tough guy face on, I put on my pre-Facebook *troll* face on and gave the guy a half smile/half chuckle and explained to him, *"It's a signal."* The guy did his best to mad dog me, then I said it again, troll face in full effect. *"It's a signal."* Then I drove off laughing with my girlfriend.

The idea behind my lame explanation is that I had deliberately left the cup on the ground not to litter, but to leave it there as some sort of signal for somebody else. Whether or not the ugly dude understood or believed me didn't matter. The important thing was I defied him, did what I wanted and avoided an altercation. That was a *win* in my book.

16. MALL COP-OUT

*E*very male wants to be *wanted* by females. Every male wants to be *envied* by other males. It's just human nature. It's man's *sinful* nature. Most guys want to be seen with a hot chick. It makes them feel important. A lot of times they treat women as an accessory that enhances their *image*. I was never like that. I treated most women who would give me the time of day, like a princess. I said "most" because there were at least two that I could've treated better, even though I didn't necessarily treat them bad. I never saw any girl as an accessory, even though I have to admit that when I first started dating, it felt good to be going out in public holding hands with a decent-looking girl. It made me appreciate relationships. It felt good to be *in* the game, for a change, rather than watching from the sidelines. I've always been the romantic type. I listened to love songs and would get all sentimental and stuff. And I love to hold hands. I learned that these were traits that worked only if you're the ultimate stud and all women wanted you. If you're anything less, then those very same traits would work against you. You'd be seen as insecure or needy.

I didn't play that game, though. If I want to be with someone, I'm *not* going to play it cool. If the girl is worth anything, I won't ever need to play it cool. I should've known that when I first got into the dating scene. The right woman will take you as you are. You can be 100% yourself and not worry about scaring them off. My advice to younger guys is that if you need to change *anything* about yourself to win a woman over, then she's not worth it. It may sound harsh or like I'm oversimplifying it, but it's true. If you need to be something other than who you *really* are to get a girl's approval, then you're *not* the guy for her. Save yourself the heartache and move on.

And if a girl treats you like crap, cheats on you and breaks up with you, then that would be a pretty good indicator that she's probably not *the one*. Anna, the very first girlfriend I ever had, was that. She cheated on me at least once and she never seemed content to be with me. She used me in so many ways. It's worth mentioning that she was not saved, and I already was at the time. Young believers, please take the Bible seriously when it instructs us not to be *unequally yoked with a non-believer*. That passage is not exclusive to romantic relationships but most definitely includes it. Light has no fellowship with *darkness*, and when a Christian gets romantically involved with a non-Christian, all hell will break loose sooner or later. For starters, you are *already* in disobedience to the Lord by getting involved with an unbeliever. Your walk will be compromised and even if it doesn't, you can bet that you will be attacked spiritually from all directions and your life can end up becoming really *miserable*. Anna was drama for all eight months our relationship lasted. Those eight months felt like an eternity in part because it was my very first relationship and in part because it *sucked*. During those eight months we broke up a total of *14 times*. I actually counted. I don't remember every incident, but I do know that at some point I started counting just for the heck of it. Thirteen out of the fourteen breakups were initiated by Anna. We kept getting back together for reasons I never should've allowed. But the fourteenth and final breakup was *my* doing. It finally hit me that I shouldn't be with anyone who was not a Christian. When I told her it was over, it was *over*.

She tried to get back together a few times to no avail. One of those times happened shortly after I started talking to another girl. Her name was Laura. We weren't exactly dating yet, but we had definitely expressed our interest in each other. It was a budding romance for sure. Then on one fateful Sunday morning, Anna called me and begged me to take her to the mall. I was in a very good mood that morning and I didn't feel like rejecting her. Just because we were broken up it didn't mean that I had to be a *jerk* to her. There was nothing harmful in taking anybody to the mall to hang out. There's nothing wrong with being *just* friends. Oh, and here's another bit of advice to all you youngsters. There's no such thing as "just friends" when it comes to the opposite sex. I'm not going to elaborate at this time, but take my word for it. Don't make a bunch of friends from the opposite sex. You just need one, ever, and that person should be your *spouse*.

So anyway, I pick up Anna and we go to the mall. We were having a pleasant time just enjoying each other's company, so much so that I held her hand, for old time's sake, "old time" being a couple of *weeks* prior. So there we were holding hands, walking and laughing like a couple. I'm not exaggerating when I say that less than ten seconds go by and I hear someone say, "*Hey, Chris*!" I turn my head and see *Laura* walk right past me. She was with her mother. I instantly let go of Anna's hand and literally *dove* to the ground as though someone had thrown a *grenade*. I was thinking, "Uhm hello, Laura has *already* seen you. Next time, dive for cover *before* she sees you!" So I pick myself up from the ground and look at Anna, who had this complete look of bewilderment in her face. I abandon her and chase after Laura. I catch up to her and see tears rolling down her cheeks. I did the classic, "*It's not what it looks like! I can explain!*" She didn't say a word, but her mom did. "You're a dog. But you play the sax good!" *Ouch*. I played my sax once for Laura over the phone and she really liked it. But I blew it. That was the end of Laura and me. There would be no recovering from this blunder. As for Anna, I left her at the mall. I didn't even bother looking for her. I just drove home. She eventually got a ride, from her mom, I think, and she let me have it over the phone. Laura and I weren't meant to be, and I trust that it was the Lord's will for me to not enter into a relationship with Laura. God probably spared me some drama and ended it quickly for me. It doesn't make feel any less of a jackass for getting caught in that admittedly comical situation. It's comical now, I mean, it was funny then, too, but feelings did get hurt and I broke Laura's heart. I honestly didn't feel too bad about leaving Anna at the mall, though. God's will or not, she *ruined* what I had going with Laura. Sure, ultimately it was my fault, but still.

17. FREESTYLE STUPIDITY

*B*reaking up with Anna was one of the best things that ever happened to me at that point in my life. We were in an on again, off again relationship for *eight months*. Those eight months had a few bright spots but was dominated by *darkness*. To be fair, Anna didn't have the best childhood. I'm not going to get into it at all, but it was pretty messed up. Now I'm not going to give her a pass on all the evil she did to me just because things happened to her when she was growing up. She was not a good girlfriend, period. She was downright *horrible*. But I forgive her, and I do hope that she has found the Lord. I did manage to formally preach to her once in a letter. I laid it all out for her, the *gospel*. She was sort of dismissive but did not reject it flat out. I also got to talk to her about Jesus from time to time. Hopefully the seeds landed on good soil.

At any rate, as I had previously mentioned, we broke up a total of *fourteen times*. The one and only time I broke up with her was the fourteenth. We had just gotten back together a few days earlier but it was though a light suddenly turned on in my head. It was the Holy Spirit. Perhaps I should've been listening all along and never have gotten into a relationship with Anna in the first place. Better late than never, as they say. It just suddenly became so obvious to me that a Christian should not be *unequally yoked* with a non-believer. It was a startling moment of clarity for me and I saw *everything*. I acknowledged the error of my ways and my foolishness. There was no need for me to continue in them. So I called her up and told her that we should "*cool it off*" or something like that. She did not take it well. She flipped her lid. I don't think she wanted me that badly, I think it was more her *ego*. She probably couldn't handle the fact that it was her getting *dumped* this time. Or maybe she finally realized how much I meant to her. It didn't matter. Ending that relationship was one of the wisest things I've ever done in my life. I saw the light and I wasn't about to turn back around.

After several days have gone by, I felt completely *liberated*. During those days Anna and I have been talking on the phone, still getting into arguments over stupid things, but the difference was, I had *nothing* on the line. I wasn't emotionally involved. I hate to admit it, but at that point I was basically just toying with her and getting her all worked up for no other reason than because it was *fun*. Do understand that I wasn't doing it to spite her or to be vengeful. I just really found it entertaining to mess with her and get her going over stuff I didn't care about. I was in the flesh, no doubt. My prankster side emerged. I should say, *reemerged*. Big parts of who I was were suppressed by our relationship. I felt like I was walking on eggshells the entire time. Now, I felt free to crush every single shell on my path and I could be myself again. It felt *great*. So this one Saturday night when my best friend Fritz was over, Anna called me. I don't remember how the conversation began but at some point, I pretended to get upset and I told Anna that I had bought an *engagement ring* and that I was going to go to her house that very moment and ask her to marry me. Of course it wasn't true, but I made it sound as convincing as I could. Anna completely bought it and she was upset. We were already arguing about something, which I probably started because I knew how to press her buttons. Remember that it was Anna, not me, who wanted to get back together. But in some twisted, convoluted way, I managed to turn the tables around during our phone conversation and made it seem as though I was the one trying to pursue her, but that I was playing for keeps this time. There was absolutely no logic to the case I was presenting to her. It was an emotional performance on my part, keyword "*performance*."

Fritz was doing his best to muffle his laughter in the background. I was arguing and pleading with *passion*. It confused the heck out of Anna and made her even more upset. She warned me not to show up at her doorstep. Now it was *her* pushing me away. I told her that I was going to hang up and drive straight to her home. So I hung up. Immediately the phone rang, but I didn't pick up. It rang a dozen times before she finally gave up. A few minutes later, the phone rang again. I didn't have caller ID, not sure if it was even available then, but it had to have been Anna. Over the next hour she kept on calling and each time I just let it ring. Fritz and I were just cracking up the entire time. This is what single men do in their spare time; *mess with their ex's.*

The phone rang once more and an idea popped into my head. I picked it up and answered with the angriest voice I could muster. I asked Anna, *"Why?"* And she was like, *"Why what?"* Then I said in a dramatically louder voice, *"Why did you call the police on me?"* Anna, now more confused than ever, answered, *"What are you talking about?"* It went back and forth for a short while, me accusing Anna of calling the cops on me and her denying it. Fritz was laughing but was confused himself, not sure where I was going with this. Then I basically screamed to Anna, *"The cop pulled me over for a missing license plate! Now how could he have known? He pulled me over from the back, but my missing license plate was from the front!"* Now that was the height of all the nonsense that came out of my mouth that night, and it was *fantastic*. Fritz nearly died laughing. He called what I did, *"freestyle stupidity."* And it was. Everything I said to Anna that night was spontaneous nonsense. I just went with wherever the wind blew and Anna took the bait every single time. It was too easy. I had way too much fun with her that night, and I felt she deserved all the drama. At least it was all made up.

From then on, whatever was left of our relationship/ friendship just faded and we eventually stopped talking to each other for good. We did see each other again about two years later, just to catch up on each other's lives, no strings attached. We agreed to meet somewhere near my work during my lunch and we basically just said hi and talked for a few minutes before saying goodbye to each other for the last time. I know I've said nothing good about her, and after nearly twenty years, I still can't really say anything good about her. She was who she was. One thing I will say is that in spite of it all, I really did love her deeply for the majority of the eight months we were together. She couldn't have hurt me so badly otherwise. I wish her nothing but the best.

18. BUH-BYE, SUPRA

My very first car was a 1986 Toyota Supra. I was proud of that car. I've since had newer, shinier cars but to this day, it's still *the* best car I've ever owned. I took great care of that car, kept it clean inside and outside and regularly got it maintained. I'm not a car guy at all, so when I say "maintained," I mean taking it to the nearest car place for service. I had that car for nearly seven years. I'd probably still have it today if it weren't for one fateful April morning. I was driving to Orange Coast College for one of my saxophone lessons with a *certain* saxophonist, famous in the jazz circles but not so much in the more pop-oriented crowd. He wasn't a pure traditional jazz saxophonist, but he was pretty *hardcore*. He was big in the *fusion* scene of the late 80's.

So anyway, I was stopped at an intersection near the parking lot, waiting for the left arrow to turn green. I may have been the only car making a left, I think. As I made my turn when the arrow turned green, the car on the opposite side of the intersection, which was also stopped at the red light, decided to go straight towards me. The weird thing was the car appeared to *accelerate* all of a sudden right before it hit my car, almost as though it was *deliberately* trying to hit me. It happened very quickly but my mind was processing it in slow motion. I was thinking, *"Why is this guy speeding up when he should be hitting the brakes?"* The car had *plenty* of time to stop. It was a wide intersection. I've seen countless "false starts" in my life and have committed plenty myself. You know the deal; the car across the intersection gets a green arrow and starts turning, and you instinctively let your foot off the brakes though *your* light is still *red*. You quickly realize your error and immediately slam on the brakes. Well this car just kept on *going*. Not only did the car keep going, it made no attempt at slowing down and even seemed to pick up speed in the middle of the intersection. I was completely baffled. I was even more shocked to discover that it was an older woman who was driving and not some drunk or an irresponsible *teenager*. She wasn't incredibly old, probably between her late 50s and early 60s, and when we both got out of our cars she seemed like a really decent person, very polite and calm. She had struck my car almost perpendicularly, right on the passenger's door. It spun my car around but thankfully, I was not hurt at all. I didn't even get sore in the following days as some people do after a car wreck from which they thought they walked away *unscathed*. My car wasn't so lucky. The impact didn't feel that violent to me but apparently, it hit my car at just the right spot for maximum damage. I don't know what part of the car it was exactly, but if I recall correctly it may have been the frame that absorbed all the force. Whatever it was, my car got *totaled*. That was the last time I ever got to drive my Supra.

The interesting thing was that my dad just renewed my car insurance the day prior. Immediately after the collision, I had what I would consider *perfect peace* about the situation. I was not the least bit upset about my car or the possibility that it may have been destroyed, which it turned out it was. The timing of the car insurance getting renewed and the fact that I was completely unharmed gave me the assurance that God allowed this to happen for *His* own reasons, and that I could trust Him in this whole situation. Count it as another "*God moment*" for me. I'm not proud to admit it, but even after I became a Christian, I've profaned God's name over much lesser things than a totaled car. But on this particular day, I had *victory*. I didn't have a single complaint in my heart. I thanked God for his protection and provision. Physically I was alright and legally I was covered. He ordained this moment for reasons that to this day I still don't know. Then my dad came to pick me up. We waited until the remains of my Supra got towed away. On the way home, my dad suggested that I should get checked out to make sure I'm *really* okay. I told him that it wouldn't be necessary. I hardly felt a jolt during the impact. I was fine. After I said that, my dad *insisted* that I should get checked out because it wasn't uncommon for people to suffer internal injuries without knowing it. There may have been wisdom in my dad's advice, but my physical wellbeing was the last thing on his mind.

He saw the car accident as a *financial opportunity*, to perhaps be able to get some insurance money out of it. He knew the *dance*. By going to a clinic, I would have a paper trail. Maybe I could even go through physical therapy as a precautionary measure. It would strengthen my case. My dad argued that if I didn't take these steps, the woman I got in a crash with would, and should she try to sue me, I would be a sitting duck. I wouldn't have any of it. I was going to trust the Lord on this and will not resort to any type of deception. The minute I do, I would be forfeiting the Lord's protection on the matter and would have to rely on my own wits. No thanks. My dad was fuming for most of the drive home as I refused to cooperate with his schemes. He yelled at the top of his lungs, eyes bulging out as he cussed up a *storm*. It was a small miracle that we didn't get into an accident. He attacked and mocked my faith and called me all sorts of degrading names for wanting to walk the straight and narrow path. I stood my ground and did not budge.

After all was said and done, I was right; my body was unharmed from the accident. Life went on. My dad didn't get whatever money he thought he could've gotten out of this ordeal. I refuse to use deception or play the games the world makes people play to get ahead in this life. Perhaps the obvious result is that I've not gotten ahead at all in this life. I've essentially been walking on a treadmill. I can't say that I'm not disappointed because I am quite disappointed in myself and have plenty of regrets. One of the regrets I do *not* want on my list is willfully disobeying the Lord for personal gain. Whatever I gain from that will not be worth the sleep I lose over it.

19. INVALIDATED

*O*ver the course of three years, I took private saxophone lessons from a world-renowned saxophonist. I'm actually very proud of this. The guy is awesome, absolutely one of the best. He's a phenomenal sax player and an absolute machine. The reason he didn't achieve real fame is because his songwriting didn't really click with the masses. Still, I always saw him as the *Michael Jordan* of saxophonists. I admit that's a bit of an exaggeration on my part, but he's without a doubt among the best in the *world*. He's a consummate professional. Besides having numerous solo albums and collaborations with other musicians, he has done saxophone work in movies, TV shows and commercials. Two things I give him credit for are first and foremost, developing my technique through disciplined practice. He taught me *how* to practice. Second, he gave me confidence in my own abilities. It's very important for any musician to believe in his craft regardless of what others may think, especially in an industry filled with critics.

It's probably been twenty years since I last saw him and one of these days I'd love to be able to meet up with him again just so I can *fanboy* all over again. For obvious biased reasons, I really was a fanboy when I was taking lessons with him, though none of the people I knew really cared since not too many people were into jazz or *smooth* jazz. It didn't stop me from bragging about being his student. One of the venues he regularly performed at was a restaurant called *Spaghettini's*. He invited me to come to one of his shows and I did. I took my dad with me. We sat next to a couple of men who looked kinda like big shots. They were the richer, upper class CEO type. You could tell by how they dressed, how they talked, and how their hair was styled. But on that night, they were simply *fans*. Now I'm not the guy to engage in small talk. In fact, I *hate* the heck out of small talk. I only talk about things that I'm truly interested in. It just so happened that I'm truly interested in jazz and saxophone. So, just like a normal person, a rare occurrence for me, I struck up a conversation with them. I wasn't bothered by the fact that they were several rungs up the social ladder from me. They were probably in their late 40s, living the *dream*. And there I was, in my twenties just barely getting started in life and *jobless* at the time, chatting with them like we were *equals*. I was in my *element*. Naturally, at some point in the conversation I brought up the fact that I was one of his students. Color them *impressed*. They even shared their *appetizers* with me. I was quite the big man.

So we watched the concert and I was really into it, grooving and bobbing my head to the beat. When the first set was over, my sax teacher came down from the stage and started greeting people from table to table and was making his way over to ours. I briefly made eye contact with him and gave him a little wave, I don't remember for sure whether or not he gave me an acknowledging nod, but he just kept on *walking*. I figured he must've been headed to the bathroom. Surely he'd come back to sit down with one of his *prized* students. But he never did. He just went back up on stage and started the second set. After that, the two rich dudes just gave me this look of disapproval and didn't say another word to me the rest of the night. They were probably expecting to meet my sax teacher through me, but he treated me like a stranger. I'm pretty certain they thought I'd been lying to them the entire time. I didn't really care what they thought, but I was extremely disappointed that the guy I looked up to and basically put on a pedestal, just straight up ignored me. All I wanted was some validation, but I guess I wasn't worthy of any. On a positive note, on the very next lesson I had with him, I believe it was just a few days later, he thanked me for showing up to his gig and sincerely apologized for not being able to take a minute to hang out. He even went out of his way to introduce himself to my dad, who drove me to the lesson as I still didn't have a replacement car for my *totaled* Supra. He was very cordial to my dad and expressed his appreciation for showing up at his concert. He praised me for being a good student.

Today when I look back to that incident at Spaghettini's, I could still feel a little bit of the embarrassment and disappointment I experienced. It was a *huge* deal to me at the time. But then I think of how much worse it would be for a person who *thinks* he's a Christian, to one day meet Jesus only to hear the words, "*I never knew you.*" There are countless people out there who walk around thinking they are right with God but are far from it. They may believe they're a Christian but in reality have never been truly born again. "*I never knew you.*" Those are words you *never* want to hear from the Lord. Don't be that guy.

If you are unsure of your standing with God, you can be sure today, right this very moment. First, think about the Ten Commandments. Have you ever lied? Have you ever lusted after a woman or a man? Have you ever *hated* anyone? Chances are, as in 100%, the answer to those questions is *yes*. If you've ever lusted after another person, Jesus said you are *guilty* of adultery. If you've ever had hatred in your heart towards another, Jesus counts that as *murder*. The Bible teaches that if you break just one commandment, you are guilty of breaking them *all*. You are guilty. We *all* are. We don't stand a chance on Judgment Day. We all deserve *hell*. Understand this. *You deserve hell*. If you're not right with God, if you died today you will go straight to hell. That's the bad news.

The good news is, God made a way for each and every single one of us to escape hell. He gave us exactly one way, and that way is Jesus. Jesus is God becoming man for the sole purpose of dying on the cross to pay the penalty of our sins. He rose physically from the dead on the third day. What you need to do is *repent* of your sins, then turn towards the Lord and put your faith in Him, 100%. Ask for His forgiveness and put your faith in His completed work on the cross. You know the famous passage. John 3:16 says, "*For God so loved the world that He gave His only begotten son, that whosoever believes in Him shall not perish but have everlasting life.*" Take Him at His word. By doing so, you can rest assured that if you died today or in a hundred years, you will spend eternity in heaven, in the Lord's presence.

20. (JUST DON'T) PREACH IT, BROTHER

*P*aul the apostle said that he was untrained in speech, but not in knowledge. I kinda feel that way about myself. I'm not a good speaker. Part of it is having an unsophisticated *vocabulary*. The best speakers can embellish the simplest phrases and make them sound so profound. I'm like the opposite of that. I can talk about the most profound ideas and make them sound so *ordinary*. I can carry on one-on-one conversations with no problem (depending on the topic, of course). I consider myself a pretty good listener, and I found that if you genuinely tune in to what the other person is saying and show interest, they can practically have a conversation with themselves while you just stare and nod. That, right there, is truly *profound*, but I bet I made it sound like there's nothing to it. There's a *lot* to it. It really isn't as simple as staring and nodding. You have to internally build interest on what the other person is talking about. You also have to be prepared for the occasional "quiz," where the other person would actually ask for your opinion and stop talking for a little while. You had better be prepared to give some feedback. Also, most people know if you're BS-ing them. Sometimes they don't care; they just want someone to *listen* to them, or even to *pretend* to listen to them. But more often than not, they want someone who *cares*. The real skill here is the art of making yourself care, even just for the moment.

Most people love to talk about themselves and the things they like. I, on the other hand, know that nobody really cares about the things I'm into, so I've learned over the years to just *shut up*. I don't like being patronized, and I don't like putting others in the position to have to do that to me. I don't want to force them into having to *lie* about wanting to hear what I have to say. It's one thing when I'm the one doing the listening, because like I said, one of my skills is making myself actually care *on the spot.* But other people don't have this skill and would have to resort to talking out of their *butts*. I'm not a dog. I don't like sniffing rear ends, let alone having *conversations* with them. I especially hate it when older family members who fancy themselves as intellectuals, try to converse with me about video games. They think they can engage me in an intelligent exchange of ideas and opinions regarding video games. They *can't*. I actually find it quite offensive because I think it's so condescending. They speak in broad strokes and don't really know what the heck they're talking about. They view gamers as mental midgets who are so desperately seeking the approval of the likes of them. They think that by showing even the *slightest* hint of interest in video games, they could get our engines going. Kinda like throwing a crumb of bread on the pier and expecting a flock of seagulls to just start raining down from the sky to get a piece of that scrap. *Seagulls*. That's what they think of gamers as. Thanks, but no thanks. Don't want their conversation. Like I said, I don't talk to *butts*.

I do talk to people though. I prefer talking to individuals when it comes to the topic of the Lord. I like to be able to get a chance to really understand what they're thinking and be able to provide satisfactory answers to each and every question. There was a time when I was all into apologetics. I could never turn down a good *debate*. I felt like I knew magical kung fu or something. I had all the right moves and counters and could refute just about every heresy and overcome any objection. It's important to know the Word of God and to learn apologetics from those who were given greater understanding by the Lord. The Bible instructs us to have a *ready defense* to everyone asking for an account concerning the *hope* that is in us. However we can't let apologetics be the end all, be all. There's a certain satisfaction to "checkmating" unbelievers and having an answer for everything they throw at you, but that is all *flesh*. It's *not* what the Gospel is all about. It's about getting inside people's hearts and making them aware of their desperate *need* for a Savior, not to make their earthly lives better, but to escape God's *judgment*. I've preached to quite a few people since I got saved over twenty years ago, though probably not nearly as many as I should've.

I'm not through yet, and I still long for opportunities to talk to people about the Lord. One thing I know, though. If I had it my way, it would *not* be in front of a group. I tried that *once*.

And it wasn't even a full-fledged attempt. It was during my stint at a community college, after I had already flunked out of Cal State Long Beach. It was for a music class. Each of us had to talk about either a musical group or genre in front of the whole class. I really don't remember too many details about my presentation. I know that I've forgotten countless details that I wish I could recall in a lot of my stories, but this is one of the few stories I actually wish I could just erase from my memory. Unfortunately, it remains intact in my head. I seriously don't know what my personal objective was, but I decided to talk about this obscure, Christian *hip-hop* group. I forget (*surprise, surprise*) what the group's name was, but I bought their CD at a Christian bookstore. Musically, they weren't half bad. They had a great sound and were basically indistinguishable from secular hip-hop groups in terms of the quality of the production. Of course rather than talking about sex, drugs, bling or murder, this group talked about the Lord. The general theme of their album was repentance, particularly for the backslidden believer. Anyway, I talked about this group in front of my class, which thankfully wasn't that big, consisting of maybe 30 people max. The whole point of my speech was that this musical group was so *radical* and "*offensive*," that radio stations won't play their music. In my head, it was supposed to be somehow connected to how the Gospel of Jesus Christ is treated by the world as a whole. Then at some point during my speech, I would put it all together to make that point, about how the Gospel is *suppressed* and opposed by our society. I had envisioned my speech to be a mic drop that would make the people in the classroom realize how the devil is keeping everybody away from the Gospel. My speech accomplished *none* of that. If any point got across at all, it was nothing more than the hip hop group not getting any airtime on the radio; you know, like the *thousands* of other aspiring musicians out there. Yup, truly earth-shattering, eye-opening stuff.

It was a complete fail in my eyes. I know that sometimes you do the stupidest things for the Lord and you have the best of intentions and things don't pan out the way you hoped they would, but down the road, you'll discover that God used that very thing you thought was a failure for His glory. I can assure you, this was *not* one of those situations. It was just stupid.

God didn't get any glory from this and never will. It was just plain lame. I'm just not called to be the type of speaker that would move the hearts of the masses. It's a gift that I simply don't have.

21. DANCED LIKE EVERYBODY'S WATCHING

When I look back to the last few decades, I'd say that a lot, if not the majority of the most embarrassing moments of my life involved my music. As I explained before, it's because I put so much of myself into my saxophone playing. For the longest time being a sax player was my identity; it was who I am. It's the only real talent that I have that most people would consider a talent. I'm not at all a professional even though some people who hear me play might say that I am. I'm good enough to fool some but not good enough for the *world stage*. Still, I am proud of the portion the Lord has given me and will be grateful for the rest of my life.

I do have one *Godzilla*-sized complaint with my music, however. For as long as I've been playing, I never had the opportunity to play with a group that plays my style of music. My favorite style is *smooth jazz*. I'd love to be a part of a smooth jazz band. A close second would be an R&B/funk-style group. I admit that I probably could've done more to seek out these types of bands, but it wasn't like I just sat there waiting for one to come knocking at my door. After my rookie years playing with *Main Course*, a party band specializing in pop songs old and newish, I got to play with three other bands. One was a Christian band whose musical style is beyond classification. The other two were the worship bands from a couple of churches I attended over the years. They played almost exclusively rock music. Rock and sax don't really go together, although some may argue otherwise. I did what I could and I made it work to the best of my ability. It did sound good for the most part, but it still wasn't the perfect fit. To me it was like being a formula one car being forced to drive on a *dirt track*.

I did have this one-off opportunity to play in a Gospel/R&B group. In college, I met this guy with a phenomenal voice. He had that *Boyz II Men* type of style, and we became pretty good acquaintances for a *season*. During that time we decided to participate in a Gospel-themed concert at our college, where various groups were invited to perform. We put together a ragtag band on short notice. The songs we practiced were all originals, one of them being mine. We sounded OK, I guess, and even though our rhythm section was a bit lacking, my friend's strong lead vocals backed up by my passionate sax licks more than made up for it. We had a blast during the 10 or 15 minutes we spent on stage. The audience seemed to enjoy it as well. It was, to put it simply, a *success*. We were proud of the work we did. The thing about me is that being naturally shy, *showmanship* has never been my strong suit. I've learned to break out of that and have become much, much looser as a *performer*. Early on, however, whenever I played in front of an audience, I basically just stood on one spot and barely moved. For this concert, however, I was feeling it. I was playing the style of music I'm into and playing with my peers who were on the same *wavelength* as I was. I did more than just stand one spot. I *dipped* my knees to the beat as subtly as I possibly could have. My parents and my uncle watched the show. Afterwards when they greeted me, my uncle approached me and dipped his knees repeatedly in mockery of what I did on stage. I basically ignored him, refusing to let him ruin my moment. Not only did our band do fantastic, I also had a pretty blonde *in my arm* (just one of the few unofficial girlfriends from my past).

I wasn't fazed by my uncle's antics. On a side note, this was the very same uncle who caught me looking at the nudie magazine my dad brought home one time when I was a little kid. He actually bullied me throughout my childhood and part of my young adulthood, until I started standing up to him when I was big enough to take him. I still loved on him, however, especially after I got saved. I regularly preached the *Gospel* to him. Sadly, he died relatively young from a rare disease. His final years weren't the best, but I did manage to lay out the Gospel to him one last time, in the form of a letter, which covered every detail I could think of. He read it during one of his stays at the hospital and was so uplifted by it that he shared the letter with the nurses. I can only wonder if he ever got right with the Lord before he died, but I'm thankful that I was faithful to have done my part.

So at any rate, there's a fair chance that I could've looked more than a little silly on stage, doing that knee-bobbing thingy. You see, I danced like everybody was watching, which they were, and since then I've learned to dance like nobody was watching, as the late, great *Satchel Paige* is famously quoted for. It actually works out better that way; you're more likely to dance good enough in front of people when you're pretending they're not there, as opposed to dancing like they were there, which could result in stiffer movements. Capeesh?

22. RECORDING ARTIST

*K*enny G came along at the perfect time and era. The sax was a *hot* commodity in the 80s and played a prominent role across varying styles of music, from pop to rock and everything in between. Kenny G was the perfect package. He had the right look, the right personality and the right set of skills to make him stand out from the pack. Love him or hate him, he is *the* most successful instrumentalist of *all time* and is unlikely to ever be surpassed. He appealed to the masses because simply put, he made beautiful music that *regular* folk could appreciate. Also, despite what bitter jazz purists might say about Kenny G, the man could *play*. He was also able to capitalize on an opportunity to become a global star and managed to stand shoulder to shoulder with the top artists of an industry dominated by vocalists. Many saxophonists have come and gone since the Kenny G era of the 90s and achieved some degree of fame, but none have come close to replicating his success.

Playing the sax was one of the biggest passions I've ever had, but I always knew that I didn't have the talent, looks or personality to ever become *famous*. But for a time I did want to become a *professional*. There's nothing better than making a living out of something that you'd gladly do for free. The reality though, is that there simply aren't too many career options for a saxophone player. The obvious path is to join a band that can land steady *gigs*. There are only two types of bands; those that must continually look for work, and those that people *pay* to see. If I ever made it in the industry in *any* capacity, it would've been the former. There are plenty of musicians who never achieve fame or real fortune but make a decent living. I am good enough to have been one of those. Had I tried harder there's more than a good chance I could've eventually found the perfect band to join. But as a Christian, I knew that the road a musician must travel is filled with compromises and *temptations*. There's just this feeling of darkness whenever I imagine myself being a professional musician. Countless hours spent on the road, staying at different hotels several nights a week and, uhm, meeting women along the way would be the norm. You don't have to be a rock star to attract the opposite sex. People are naturally drawn to *performers* whether or not they're famous. It's ultimately a numbers game. Sooner or later, you will strike someone's fancy and they will strike yours. It's *chemistry*. It's human nature. It's man's *sinful* nature. So while I do like to daydream about being a successful sax player, performing on stage and impressing the heck out of everyone, I knew that there was a much darker side to it all. Deep down inside, that's what really kept me from pursuing a musical career.

Success in the entertainment industry, perhaps more than any other industry, relies on *networking*. It's about connections. First and foremost, you have to have the *goods*. There's no getting around that. But having the ability is only half the battle. You have to know the right *people*. I'm not even talking about the big time here. I'm talking small opportunities to showcase your skills, oftentimes without any monetary compensation. You do it to *"get your name out there."* Do that frequently enough and you hope that eventually someone will be watching who suddenly realizes they have a need for the specific set of skills you have. That never happened to me. The most exposure I ever got was playing for my church's worship team for about a year and a half. It was decent-sized church, by no means a mega-church, but definitely big enough and popular enough to have seated a band member or some sort of producer on one of the Sundays I played. I've been complimented a few times by strangers after a service, but that's it; no producers offering me a sax part in their latest project and nobody from a band telling me that they could use a sax player like me.

But there was this one time in college that I got hooked up with an aspiring hip hop producer. Someone from my class told me that his buddy needed a sax player to record a line or two, and I took the opportunity. His studio was set up in his home, and he did have a pretty fancy setup with lots of different consoles and flashing lights. What he wanted me to do was play the sax solo from *Careless Whisper*, perhaps the most iconic sax solo in the history of pop music. He was going to incorporate it into some hip hop track he was working on. So I did my thing and he recorded it. He was actually quite pleased with my work. He said something like, *"You play the dopest sax!"* Or it could've been *"You're the dopest sax player."* I don't remember exactly. For all I know he could've said, *"You play sax like a dope!"* At any rate, I was in and out of there in less than 20 minutes. To my surprise, as I was about to walk out the door, he stopped me for a second and pulled a twenty dollar bill out of his wallet and handed it to me. *Twenty dollars for less than twenty minutes' work.* That's the highest rate I've ever been paid in my *entire life.* It made my day, and I am really proud of this little feat. It was the first and only time I ever got paid for playing my sax in a *studio.* The way I see it, it made me a recording artist, even for a day. I actually had another studio session not long after that, but with another musician. It was an aspiring female vocalist who was working on her debut album. I did a lot more work for her, with longer parts for several songs on her album. I didn't get paid for it at all. I wasn't expecting to, it was just a favor. Anyway, this girl didn't make it in the music industry. She's not famous or anything today. Just like me.

23. KARAOKE KING

I met Rochelle at Cypress College during a concert event I performed in. It's the same college as that one Gospel concert, but not the same concert. This time I was with the college jazz band and Rochelle was with the choir. I've seen her around a couple of times before. She was *strikingly* beautiful. I think I may have spoken to her sometime prior, but the conversation was nothing remarkable. I think I pretended not to know where a particular classroom was and asked her if she did. Or maybe it was her who asked me something, I don't remember. But on this occasion, I talked to her in a playful way as she was passing by. I said *hi* and confused her as she didn't know where the sound came from. It was a brief exchange. One of the girls from her choir was in one of my classes. I asked that girl to give my phone number to Rochelle. She warned me to think twice about Rochelle because she was supposedly *really* dumb. I didn't believe her nor did I care. I thought she was just *jealous* because Rochelle was super pretty and about a third her size. So she gave my number to Rochelle and Rochelle actually called me a few days later. We hit it off instantly and we started dating pretty much right away.

I'll have more to say about Rochelle later on, but for now I'd like to talk about the time we went to a karaoke bar. It wasn't exactly a karaoke bar; it was a *pizza place* that had karaoke and a dance floor. We met up with a few of her friends. I wanted to impress Rochelle because that's what cool *boyfriends* do. And I was definitely a cool boyfriend. In fact, I never felt cooler than I did when I was with Rochelle, for most of the four months that we lasted. We were like a *Hollywood* couple. Our relationship was flashy, showy, presentable and *shallow*. So I brought my tenor sax with me to the karaoke place. I loved my tenor sax. It had a great, natural tone. It's too bad that I had to sell it many years later, but I loved my tenor because it was much easier to achieve a great sax sound with it than with my alto sax. My alto became my primary horn, though, as I got better. Anyway, I'm not sure how common it was for musicians to bring their instruments to a karaoke bar, but I always saw the sax as the closest thing to the human voice any instrument can come. I can't sing, so why not bring my sax? The DJ was a bit surprised but was totally cool with it. I brought my sax in a "*gig bag*" rather than a case. For the uninitiated, a gig bag *is* a carrying case, except that it's sort of shaped like a sax and has a strap that allows you to sling it over your shoulder. It makes you look a lot cooler than when you're lugging around a regular case like a band geek. It also makes you look like an accomplished musician who knows what's he's doing.

The song I picked to play was none other than "Careless Whisper." It was a popular song that has aged gracefully, being nearly twenty years old at the time. So we sat at the table and ordered pizza as I awaited my turn. I did my best not to attract too much attention as I was putting my horn together. I was finally called to the stage and I *rocked* "Careless Whisper" like a total pro. I was feeling it, styling and grooving to the music, much better than I did at the Gospel concert when I was just dipping my knees like a moron. I felt like a *star*. It was one of my best performances ever, and the crowd *loved* it. After I was done, Rochelle and I engaged in a little bit of PDA, not too excessive, just a little something for the *cameras* because that's the kind of couple we were. Then we went to the dance floor and started dancing. It was one of the first *sobering* moments I had about Rochelle. She danced like she was trying to be *funny*. She's a hot chick, and she dressed like a hot chick. She turned heads wherever she went. She was a trophy girlfriend. But at that moment she looked like an *idiot*. I can only describe what she was doing as *voguing*, if it was performed by a partially reanimated corpse. It was *bad*. The girls around us literally stopped dancing to stare at her to try to figure out what the heck it was she was attempting to do. I did my best to hide the embarrassment, keeping a straight face with a tiny hint of a smile as I waited for it to be over. It did finally end, and in spite of Rochelle's dancing, it was still a pretty fantastic night for me. I did great on my sax. By the way, from this point on, I'd like to refer to Rochelle as "*Dumb Rochelle.*" It is a bit cruel, but I have to make a distinction between this Rochelle and another Rochelle I'll be telling you about later.

24. DUMBER THAN DUMB

About a month before I met *Dumb* Rochelle, I met *another* Rochelle. This Rochelle and I became really close friends in such a short period of time. She was something special. We saw each other eye to eye and just understood each other. We'd spend hours talking on the phone almost every night, talking about nothing and everything. She became my confidant. After Dumb Rochelle and I started officially dating, I told Rochelle about her. It turns out that they knew each other from way back when. They weren't close friends or anything, but they were both part of some school-related group that got together on a regular basis. I was complaining to Rochelle about Dumb Rochelle and about the weird stuff that she does. It didn't take long for Rochelle to realize it was the same Dumb Rochelle she knew. Everything I said about Dumb Rochelle checked out. Once Rochelle got a positive ID on Dumb Rochelle, she started making fun of me. I couldn't argue with Rochelle because Dumb Rochelle was wrong for me in so many ways. In fact, there are not too many men on this planet she'd be right for. The novelty of Dumb Rochelle's *supermodel* looks could only go so far. I was proud of the fact that an ugly dude like me could land a girlfriend like her, but Dumb Rochelle had the IQ of a third grader, which explained a *lot*. No offense to third graders, but adults are supposed to have *adult* brains. At best, I was putting up with Dumb Rochelle and being as loving as I possibly could. At worst, I was *miserable*.

Rochelle wasn't *evil* like Anna, but she wasn't a good girlfriend either. Besides having the maturity of an 8 year-old, she wasn't faithful. I don't mean that she slept with guys and stuff, but she was a big *flirt*. She wasn't deliberately unfaithful, just *stupid*. She'd give every guy the time of day. She couldn't help herself. Meanwhile, I was falling in love with the *other* Rochelle. No, scratch that. I was *already* in love with the other

Rochelle. She was my best friend. It was classic romantic comedy material, I tell you. I remember one particular phone conversation we had in June. It was the night before she went away to New Mexico to stay with her aunt for most of the summer. It was one of the saddest nights of my life and I could tell that Rochelle wasn't too happy either. That night, I wanted to tell Rochelle so badly that I was in love with *her*, even though I was in a relationship. The words were on the very tip of my tongue but I didn't let it out, at least not on that night. So Dumb Rochelle had me all to herself for the next couple of months. How we lasted that long I couldn't tell you. I was the one carrying the relationship for sure. I was the one doing the putting up, which I don't hold against her since I made a vow to myself to never break anybody's heart, even if it cost me a lot of *pain*.

Truth be told, Dumb Rochelle didn't cause me too much pain because I didn't like her that much. She was drama but I never really had strong feelings for her. Our relationship started out great but then she showed her *true* colors. I should've broken up with her less than a month into our relationship. She would've been fine. I don't think she even had the *capacity* to be hurt. I mean, that would take average brain power, which she didn't have. Lucky her, there's a minimum amount of intelligence necessary to process emotional pain. I know I really sound like a jerk the way I'm describing her. How I *wish* I'm merely being a jerk, but I'm being completely honest. Dumb Rochelle was *dumb*. The only person *dumber* than her was *me*. I desperately wanted to end the relationship so what did I do? I asked her to *marry* me. You read that right. Before I go any further, let me explain my thought process behind all this. I told the Lord how much I wanted out, but that I had made a commitment. I was *not* going to walk away. So basically I asked the Lord to either change my *heart* or change Dumb Rochelle. I told God that I would leave this in His hands. So I went out to propose, and she said *yes*. I believe it was sometime in September. By that time, the *other* Rochelle had already returned from New Mexico and I was able to share the "good news" with her.

That's another conversation I will not forget. When I was telling Rochelle about getting engaged to Dumb Rochelle, it had about as much excitement as telling her I was terminally ill. It was a solemn conversation. Rochelle sounded pretty sad as well. There was no enthusiasm whatsoever. One thing you need to know about our friendship is that I've been somewhat open about my feelings towards her, even though I'd present it in a joking manner. I'd always tease Rochelle about her becoming my girlfriend *someday*, and she never would play along. She would always reject me, albeit in a playful way. At the same time, she never actually tried to discourage my romantic advances. I sensed that she had feelings for me even though she refused to admit them. So when I told her about the engagement, it was clear that the news *saddened* her.

But God is faithful. Two weeks later, three at the most, Dumb Rochelle *broke up* with me. It was the Lord's answer to my leap of *stupid*. It was like the greatest day of my life. I had to *pretend* to be heartbroken. To even look halfway convincing, I had to put on the absolute best performance of my life. Lucky for me, Dumb Rochelle broke up with me over the phone. No way would I've been able to hide the smile across my face had she done it in person. That would've been awkward.

PART 4: AFTER COLLEGE

*T*he title of this section is a bit of a misnomer as it might suggest that I *finished* college. I didn't. One of the reasons I'm going with this heading is to stay with the theme. First part was elementary school, then high school, then college. What comes after college? Just *everything*. For most people, *real life* begins after college. There's nothing mysterious about "real life." Real life happens when you start providing for yourself rather than relying on your parents or anyone else. Real life happens when you discover that there are real *consequences* to your actions. By these criteria some of the stories you're about to read don't even qualify to be in this section. The honest truth is that the stories I've filed under this category are some of the things that changed me forever in ways that I don't even realize. Now don't get too excited because like everything else that you've read so far, none of it will be too profound. They're mostly *girl-related* stuff. To be more specific, mostly *Rochelle*-related stuff. And I'm not talking about dear old *Dumb* Rochelle, but the *other* Rochelle, whose permanent designation will not be "the other" by the time I'm done talking about her. Until that big *reveal*, from this point on I will simply refer to her as *Rochelle*. She was a big part of my life. When she was in my life, she was *the* biggest part. She was bigger than that. She was *everything*. Prior to Rochelle, I've never loved anybody nearly as much as I loved her. And when it was all over, part of me died. The Lord was with me the entire time and He kept me propped up through it all. But after Rochelle broke up with me, I was never the same, for better or worse.

But life went on. I moved on. *Eventually*. For a season I felt like I was wandering in the wilderness the way the Israelites did when they were being led by Moses. I was just waiting for my promised land. But good things came, stupid things came, ordinary things came. Life returned to normal and life was just being *life*. From my mid-20s on, I began to accept that my life wouldn't be extraordinary, and that if I were destined to achieve any kind of greatness, it would've already happened. No kid ever starts off dreaming about becoming an ordinary person when they grow up. Kids always hope to *make a difference* one day. That's like one of the buzz phrases kids get beat over the head with for years. Teachers and parents always encourage kids to "make a difference." The thing is, everybody makes a difference, *literally*. But when kids dream about making a difference, it's not just any kind of difference, but one that could impact countless lives for the better. Kids want to grow up to be *somebody*, as I did when I was a kid. I always thought that I had it in me, until after my college years, when I came to terms with *reality*. At best, I was *ordinary*. I decided to be content with doing ordinary things, getting an ordinary job and having an ordinary *existence*.

It's funny how you spend most of your childhood dreaming big. When you get to high school, the possibilities seem endless. You have this feeling that something great awaits behind the door. Then reality hits. You find out that you're not as smart as you thought you were. For years you've put off putting any serious thought or planning behind how you'd possibly go about achieving something big. You're saving it for last. Then you finally reach that point and the wheels in your head start turning and you quickly realize that after all this time, you've got *nothing*—no ace up the sleeve, no hail Mary pass and no knockout punch. Then you just sort of go with it and hope to God that you're wrong, and that He may yet have something fabulous in store for you in *this* life. *This* is what life after college was all about for me. It is the realization of squandered opportunities and the undying hope of scoring that buzzer-beating 3-pointer to win the game. Life after college is the rest of my life.

1. THE WEDDING GIG

When I first met Rochelle's mother in person, I gave her a floppy handshake. Her mom teased her about it for a while, referring to me as *"fish hands."* Have I told you that I'm socially awkward? I deliberately gave her mom a soft handshake as a sign of respect or even *submission*. I always thought that the firm handshakes were the equivalent of staring each other down, to test each other's might and see who was the *bigger man*. So I wasn't going to have any of that when I met Rochelle's mom. No, I was going to be polite, humble and present the *softest* hands imaginable. It turned out to be all the wrong approach. This was a woman who drank black coffee. She's been through stuff in life and looked much older than she really was. Her life was one big *callous*. She required *vice grip* handshakes. Now I don't know if that's what started it all or if it was just plain bigotry (Rochelle and her family are white), but Rochelle's mom *never* liked me. In fact, she *hated* me in a passive aggressive kind of way. She'd say subtle things to insult me and she would downplay any positive topic that I would bring up at dinner conversations. She resisted the friendship that was turning into something more between Rochelle and me.

It was a little strange, actually. Rochelle's mom was generally a *domineering* woman. She wore the pants in the house, as they say. Rochelle's dad was quiet and mumbled to himself most of the time. But for a woman of such great authority, I wondered why she didn't simply tell Rochelle to stop seeing me, period. Rochelle was a good daughter and would've obeyed. I think Rochelle's mom didn't want to come across as a straight up bigot or be seen as the villain. She wanted to preserve the *illusion* of being the loving mom who was looking out for her daughter's best interest. She didn't want to be seen as the *evil queen* trying to keep the princess locked up from the valiant prince. For this reason Rochelle's mom hamstrung her own powers and had to walk a fine line.

Before Rochelle and I started dating, I would visit her at Cypress College after her classes were done. We would meet up for only minutes at a time before she had to drive home. Just a friendly reminder, I'm not talking about *Dumb* Rochelle any more, just *Rochelle*. And yes, they both went to Cypress College as well. And do allow me to back up a little. The night Dumb Rochelle broke up with me, I felt like I had won the lottery. I immediately called up Rochelle and told her the *good news*. I also professed my love for her that same night. I started by warning her that she might not want to speak to me ever again after hearing what I was about to tell her. Prior to this particular conversation, I would occasionally joke about this topic. However, this was different. I was serious and she knew it. I entertained the idea of one day telling Rochelle exactly how I felt about her for the longest time. One of the reasons it took me so long to tell her besides the fact that I was in a relationship, was that if Rochelle turned me down in a serious conversation, it would be the end of my *dream*. But I had to wake up to reality sooner or later, and I went for it. I told her everything and how long I've been in love with her. She responded with a nonchalant, "*Oh.*" That was it. The great news was, she didn't shut me down or give me the "*I just want to be friends*" spiel. That alone encouraged me to *keep on going*. I asked if I could pay her a visit on campus, and she agreed, and it became a regular thing. On occasion I'd offer to give her a hand massage and she would accept.

But anyway, her mom wasn't thrilled. She knew that Rochelle and I were becoming closer and she really couldn't do much about it. Rochelle was nonetheless intimidated by her mom, and she didn't ever ask me to come over their house. I needed to change that. I was a man on a *mission*. I wasn't afraid to go into the castle and rescue *my* princess. I wasn't about to invite myself over, either. Rochelle played the piano fairly well. She wasn't a virtuoso or anything like that, but she could read music and play contemporary stuff. As luck would have it, my friend Bridget's mom was getting married to a longtime companion, and Bridget asked me to play my sax at the wedding, which was only a few weeks away. The first thought that came to mind was to ask Rochelle if she could accompany me on the piano. So I accepted the gig and asked

Rochelle if she could go to the wedding with me to play the piano while I played the sax. She agreed. That meant we'd have to rehearse a few times at her place. She finally invited me over and we practiced regularly at her house.

The wedding took place late October and we did great as a musical duo. The best part of it all besides being able to hang out with Rochelle at her house regularly, was that immediately after the wedding, Bridget asked me if I wanted go out with her and her friends later that evening, and take Rochelle with me. Rochelle was still basically on a leash and it would almost be asking for too much, but I asked her anyway. To my surprise, Rochelle said yes. It would've been easy for her to say no and tell me that it was getting late and that her mom wouldn't approve. I mean, that's what I was kind of expecting, I just had to try. But I was wrong, and Rochelle and I went out together that night. We weren't officially a couple, but it was essentially our first date.

2. THE TURNAROUND

Rochelle and I began to spend more time with each other, either at her house or other places. For weeks we maintained "friendship" status. I didn't bother me too much because going in, I *knew* it was going to be an *uphill* battle. What mattered was that Rochelle and I were hanging out a lot and she seemed to be really enjoying my company. In the meantime, her mother was slowly beginning to turn up the heat and was becoming a little more straightforward with her objections to our friendship. Still, she couldn't just straight up forbid Rochelle to stop seeing me. I believe that it was God Himself who was preventing Rochelle's mom from fully intervening. Her lack of assertiveness in the matter was the complete opposite of the type of person I knew her to be. God was the only logical explanation in my opinion.

For several weeks, as I went along with the friendship *façade*, I would constantly tease Rochelle that she will be mine and that her feelings for me were obvious. She would laugh it off and not fess up to it but at the same time not ever drawing the line and turning me down. So I *persisted*. Was she just toying with my heart? I didn't care. I was on a mission, remember? I was willing to go through whatever drama I had to go through if in the end I could be with Rochelle. I mentioned that whenever I visited her at the college, I would give her hand massages. One evening, Rochelle came over my place (*I was still living with my parents*) and we watched some TV. I asked if I could massage her hand and she obliged as always. Now Rochelle was no fool, innocent as she was, and it was no secret that all I really wanted to do was *hold her hand*. After a few minutes, I asked, *"Do I really need to keep on massaging your hand?"* She said, *"No."* So I stopped massaging her hand but did *not* let go. We sat there motionless, staring at the TV, holding hands and not saying a word to each other. It was a magical moment. I didn't want to ruin it by commenting. I wanted it to last *forever*. It was the first time I ever held her hand, officially. I stopped caring about what she said about our relationship at the time. She could've referred to us as *"sworn enemies,"* it wouldn't have changed the fact that there was something between us. As they say, action speaks louder than words. A few nights later, we took a stroll through an old train station in Downtown Fullerton and decided to sit on a bench for a little while. It was an unusually chilly night for Southern California, even for November. I asked her if she wouldn't mind scooting over towards me *just* for warmth's sake. She did, and I put my arm over her shoulder. After a few seconds, she put her head on my shoulder and we sat just there. I couldn't believe what was happening. Once we got up and started heading to my car, I asked if we could just make it an "official" date by holding hands until we got to the car. She said *"fine, but only this time*!*"* That marked the first time we would hold hands in public.

Now there was this yearly stage production held at the Crystal Cathedral during the holiday season called, "The Glory of Christmas," which featured live animals and stuff. I got us tickets to go there in December. On the night before, it was a Friday, Rochelle and I talked on the phone. I told her how much I was looking forward to going with her, and then she dropped the *bomb*. After weeks of spending time together, holding hands and getting closer than ever, she told me, *"I can't see myself being with you."* I was initially taken back by it, but I wasn't about to quit. So I asked her what she meant by that. She did some explaining and I don't remember much of it, except that whatever reasons she gave, *none* of them were because she wasn't interested in me or that she didn't like me or anything of the sort. She kept bringing up her mom being upset whenever the two of us got together. She couldn't really understand why. After some *"cross examination,"* I got Rochelle to admit or realize that her mom was afraid she'd fall for me. I then asked her, *"What if you did? With that be too bad?"* We kept on talking. About an hour later, these exact words came out of Rochelle's mouth: *"I could easily fall in love with you."* I replied, *"So what's stopping you?"* Then we continued to talk. We stayed on the phone for several hours that night. Before we hung up, I said, *"I love you."* It wasn't the first time I've said that to her. I've told her many times before. She'd always respond with a chuckle and say, "*Okay.*" But this time it was different. She said in the softest voice possible, "*I love you too.*" It was nothing short of a miracle in my eyes. It was a conversation that began with "*I can't see myself being with you,*" and ended with, "*I love you too.*" It was a miraculous *turnaround*. It was my come-from-behind, one-punch knockout victory; the kind of thing you'd only see in movies. The following night we went to see "The Glory of Christmas" as an official couple for the first time. It was one of the most unbelievable moments of my life.

3. THE EMBRACE

My relationship with Rochelle had its share of up and downs. The "down" part usually affected *only* me, though. Rochelle's mother did everything she could to destroy our relationship, and she went about it in a patient, *tactical* kind of way. I mentioned how I wondered why she didn't just put her foot down early on and ordered Rochelle to stop seeing me. Come to think of it, her strategy was *brilliant*. She wanted the end to be *permanent*. She would apply pressure on Rochelle in controlled portions, not to break her, but just to leave tiny impressions that are engineered to haunt Rochelle for as long as our relationship lasted. She would increase that pressure gradually over time. She slowly, but surely, made Rochelle's life *a living hell*. The genius behind it is that Rochelle ultimately associated the misery with our relationship. She reached the point where she couldn't deal with her mom's torture any longer; the only clear exit was to put an end to our romance. It became not worth it anymore for Rochelle. Anything that would make her mom stop would be an acceptable *tradeoff* for whatever wonderful thing we may have had going.

Rochelle and I lasted for just over a year, and it wasn't a whole year straight. We broke up three times over that period, which admittedly is a major improvement over the *14 times* Anna and I broke up during an 8-month span. Around a week after Rochelle and I started officially dating, she called me and said that she's been *thinking about it* a lot and that she's *prayed* about it (Rochelle professed to be a Christian, by the way), and that she thought it may be a good idea for us to break up. I wasn't convinced that she didn't love me anymore. It sounded a lot like just wanting to get her mom *off her back*. I was determined to fight for us. I asked if I could come over so we could talk in person, and she agreed. It was a Sunday evening. So I got there and things started out pleasantly enough and we hung out just like we did any other night. I don't remember the details of our talk, but we had a pretty long talk. It was a good, *productive* talk. At the end of it she admitted that she did love me and very much so, and that she wanted us to *stay together*. So I basically talked some sense into her. I was determined to keep fighting for our *love* no matter what. Deep down, the only way I would stop is if I was convinced that she didn't love me anymore or if there was *another* guy in the picture. It's a possibility that everyone who's ever been in love has to accept. Every single relationship is a gamble. There are no guarantees. You really never know what's going to happen. Everything could be perfect for 50 years but it only takes *one* wrong to undo it all. There's a hundred ways a relationship could go wrong. It's a mystery that people even *want* to be in a relationship, considering how capable relationships are in destroying lives. Most people think that it sucks to be *lonely*. There are things that are far worse. People think it's great to have so much to lose because the truth is, it is. The downside is that you could actually lose it all and the pain could be much worse than you've ever imagined. During the worst parts of the relationships I've been in, I would long for the days in which I simply felt *lonely* or bored. I'd take lonely over *pain* any day. On this Sunday night with Rochelle, however, there would be no pain.

We finished talking at midnight. Everyone else in the house has gone to bed and I figured it was time for me to go. So Rochelle walked me to the front door. We kissed goodnight. And then we embraced. She rested her head on my shoulder and we just stood there embracing at the front door. It turned into minutes. Minutes turned into hours. We held each other for *over three hours straight*. We did not want to let go. We didn't say much during those three hours. We didn't need to. It was perfect bliss. *Time stood still*. When I had realized it was after 3am we finally let go. I had to be at work in a few short hours. We didn't break up that time. In fact, it'd be *peaches and cream* for the next three months. It would be the best of times, immediately followed by the darkest of times, at least for me. But on that night, I had *everything*. I couldn't have asked for much more.

4. THE THREE BREAKUPS

*B*eing in a bad relationship is like being trapped in the middle of a burning town. When you're surrounded by flames and smoke begins to fill up your lungs, you wonder if you're going to make it. The only thing in your mind is *survival*. You don't care about whatever belongings you might be leaving behind—you just want to get out of there. Should you make it out in one piece and reach a safe distance, you can look back at the town, watch it burn and almost enjoy the spectacle of it all. The hotter and bigger and more destructive the fire, the more thankful and amazed you are that you survived at all. What was for a moment, the most terrifying experience of your life, has all of a sudden become your badge of honor. That's how I see my relationship with Rochelle. Except in this case, I'm the *town*. I went down in flames. She was guilty of *arson*. Rochelle probably sees it differently. When a relationship goes bad, it's rare that any party would admit fault. It's *always* the *other* person. That's fine. It really doesn't matter today. I do think that I've written enough about Rochelle. I mean, I really could expand on the whole Rochelle saga if I chose to, but it's not really fun to reopen old wounds. God worked it out for the good and I'm in a *fantastic* place now. So without further ado, let me quickly go over our three breakups. Spoiler warning: Rochelle did all three.

Prior to this story you just read about how the first breakup attempt was averted. Rochelle's second attempt was a lot worse for me, and she was successful. We got *engaged* a week prior. I asked her to marry me and she said yes. It was pretty official. I even talked to her dad about it and there was a big announcement in front of her immediate family. The "announcement" was really meant for just her mom, as she was the last to find out. Rochelle's sister, her sister's boyfriend and her dad all knew before her mom did. We all agreed on a day to tell her. We were all there in the living room waiting for her to come home from work. When she walked in she noticed that everybody had this funny look on their faces. It was Rochelle's dad who made the *official* announcement. Needless to say, Rochelle's mom didn't take it well. The next few days were really stressful for Rochelle and understandably so, and she couldn't take it any longer. One day when I came over her house, she refused to come out. Then her mom came out with an unusually pleasant demeanor towards me, explaining how Rochelle just "*needed some time to sort things out.*" I knew where this was going. I needed to hear it straight from the horse's mouth. So I waited. Nearly *three hours*. I sat at their doorstep for three hours waiting for Rochelle to come out. It was like the undoing of the super romantic three-hour embrace we had a few months prior. Rochelle finally came out, friendly as ever. She calmly broke up with me. No amount of smooth talking could save our relationship. I saw the *finality* written all over her face. It didn't mean that I gave up, however. I just couldn't save the relationship right there and then.

I had bought tickets for us to go to a concert that was 5 weeks away. I at least got her to agree to still go with me to the concert. We didn't see each other at all during those five weeks; actually we did, a few times, at the college. We may have talked on the phone on occasion but that was it. After 5 weeks, I picked her up to go to the concert. When we arrived at the place, we found out that it had been *cancelled*. It wasn't as though none of us had access to the news or the internet, but this somehow managed to go undetected. Had we found out beforehand, we never would've seen each other that night. Rather than taking her straight back home, we spent a good portion of the evening together. She told me how much she missed me and that she *still* loved me. We kissed very passionately that night. We got back together even though we didn't get re-engaged. The second time we broke up was in the summer, about three months later. On the evening of July 3rd, Rochelle and her mom drove out of state to take Rochelle to some Christian summer camp that was to last for a month. I saw Rochelle that same evening, and all was good. Deep down inside, however, I knew that nothing good could come out of this trip. It was all part of Rochelle's mom's plan to separate us, hopefully for Rochelle to meet some guy in camp or at least realize that there are other guys out there besides me. Rochelle and I talked regularly enough on the phone while she was away and there were no signs of trouble. During that time, I also moved out of my parents' house. I moved into an apartment with some guy I knew from church. A big part of the reason I moved out was I just *knew* that Rochelle was going to break up with me, and that I needed to be able to process it without my parents hovering. I needed the space to *hurt* properly, or else I would've exploded. I called Rochelle at the beginning of August, about a couple of days after the day she told me she'd be back. The first bad sign was that she told me she had been home for a week. When I asked her why she didn't tell me, she said that she was following her mom's advice so that she could have some time to herself and *without* me. I'm not a guy who would take crap over the phone, so I asked Rochelle if I could come over. She agreed but warned me that I wouldn't like what she had to say. You see, I prefer taking crap in person, and I got it. She broke up with me once more. It wasn't as traumatic as our first breakup, but there was something a bit more sinister about this one. It was premeditated, obviously, but unlike the first time, she seemed to be in on it and was on the same page as her mom. It felt *more* final than before, and the breakup lasted longer than before. There was complete radio silence for the *next 4 months*.

Then in December, I called her again. After a few conversations, she agreed to see me. We hung out a few times and eventually got back together, about a week before Christmas. We lasted two weeks this time. Shortly after the New Year, on a Saturday night, she broke up with me. We had agreed to go to church together that night, which we still did after the breakup. She broke up with me in her room. I tried to reason with her even though I knew it was a lost cause, even before she spoke the words that will forever resonate in my mind. When I asked her why she was doing this, she said, *"Because I can't have two boyfriends!"* That was it. It was the only situation I would accept. Unless another guy was involved I had vowed to never give up on us. A week earlier, Rochelle and I went out on a date, but she asked me to take her home early. I forgot the reason she gave me, but she *played* me that night. She was extremely sweet and kissed me nicely. It was the kiss that comes second only to the one Jesus got from Judas. A few days later when I came over her house and had Chinese food with her family, Rochelle's mom was unusually friendly to me. She asked how things were going in my life, my job, how my parents were doing, etc. Rochelle broke up with me a couple of days after that night, and I was able to put two and two together. She began seeing another guy on the same night she asked me to take her home early. She had two dates that night, and I was the appetizer. Her mom knew all about it hence her sudden friendliness towards me, knowing that I was about to be *kicked to the curb*. *"Because I can't have two boyfriends!"* After she said that, we went to church as planned, with her dad. I was hurting like I've never hurt before. I couldn't even explain the feeling. It was at that moment that I knew the Lord had taken over and was carrying me the rest of the evening, if you're familiar at all with *"Footprints in the Sand."* If you're not, the famous story is about a guy who had some dream about walking with Jesus along the seashore, represented by two sets of footprints in the sand. Then in the dream, when things weren't going great in his life, he only saw one set of footprints, and he questioned Jesus why He would leave him alone during the darkest parts of his life. Jesus then explains to him that when there were only one set of footprints, it was because Jesus was carrying him. Now this isn't exactly Scripture, but there's a lot of truth in that story. It's exactly how I felt. I sang louder in church that night than I ever have in my life. I gave it all to Jesus. I remember I had a mild cold and it made my voice just a little deeper, which made it sound better in my opinion. So that was *the* end of Rochelle and me. That was the last time we saw or spoke to each other. What she did to me was *evil*. It hurt like hell. From that day forward I referred to her as *"Evil Rochelle."* I don't really think she's an evil person, at least not anymore. I say it almost with a bit of humor, to make a distinction between the two Rochelle's—one being "dumb," the other being "evil."

5. EYE-OPENER

*I*f you've read this far, I congratulate and thank you. I appreciate the interest you've taken in my unremarkable non-adventures. By now you would probably think that I have some self-esteem issues. You're probably right, although I'm still not quite convinced that I actually have a low self-esteem. In fact, for someone who has such spectacular ineptitude in all facets of life, my self-esteem is a *skyscraper*. I have plenty of reasons to look down on myself. You could say that I am the definition of a *realist*. Everything I've accomplished in life leads to one simple conclusion; I am a *magnificently mediocre man*. You know the saying, if everyone is special, nobody is. There will come a day when this corruptible body is replaced by the incorruptible and I can be with Jesus for all eternity and be everything the Lord intended me to be. Until that day I'm nothing but a *chump*. By the world's standards, I'm a bona fide *loser*. If my physical appearance isn't enough evidence, my bank account most certainly is.

If you want to make a quick assessment of your standing in society, all you have to do is ask yourself how many people in the world would *want* to be *you*. I have very little doubt that there are plenty of men out there who would trade places with me in a heartbeat, but the second question you have to ask yourself is what kind of situation do those people have to be in to envy your life. Those two questions ought to paint a pretty accurate picture of what you really are to the *world*. As a Christian, I know that my real worth lies in the fact that number one, I was created in God's image, and two, Jesus died *for me*. What I'm worth to God is *all* that matters. It's what helps me get through this oftentimes sucky pilgrimage we call *life*. My citizenship is in heaven. For now, I'd just have to roll with the punches and go with it. Maybe God does have something better in store for me in this life, even though that's not really a Biblical promise. Jesus said that in this world we will have tribulation. Now *that's* a promise. How big or small that tribulation is could differ from person to person, but it's important to know and understand that this life isn't where it's at. We make the best of it and give glory to God.

While I know all this to be true, as a human being, I still long to be *somebody*. I wish I could glorify the Lord not just in my trials, but in *victories*. I don't have too many of those in my life. I'm really not very bright. I have clear limitations. For a long time I wrestled with that. I didn't struggle in school until my second or third year in college. Maybe I lacked drive or motivation. I'm sure I could've done better if I tried harder. Effort *is* a factor. But ultimately, we live in a world where success relies solely on one's ability to *dunk* a basketball, and the reality is that I'm too short. And yes, I meant that as an *analogy* although I really am short. I'm even shorter when it comes to life. So my point is, due to my *metaphorical* height, I have zero hope of ever *metaphorically* dunking a basketball.

Still, I've always given myself the benefit of the doubt. Maybe I was a special case and that deep down inside I'm a *genius* of some kind. Perhaps I've been pursuing all the wrong things and maybe there was that *one* thing I was made for and could truly shine in. I just needed to find that *one* thing to unlock my full *potential*. One day I did find *a* thing but rather than unlocking anything, it *sealed* my fate. I got a job at some logistics firm. The position was in the accounting department and I couldn't for the life of me understand the processes they were trying to teach me. I was there for three weeks. I felt like an idiot as I continued to struggle with the most basic steps each and every day. I simply wasn't getting it. I couldn't bear the awkwardness and embarrassment any longer, although my co-workers were actually quite polite to me. One morning before my shift began, I sat at the parking lot just *thinking*. I decided that I would tell my supervisor I was resigning. So I went in and told her I was quitting. It was God's grace. She revealed to me that she was actually going to *fire* me that very same day. She already had my final paycheck ready. I thanked her for the opportunity and I found out that my supervisor was also a Christian. She said that she's prayed about her decision to let me go and was relieved that she didn't actually have to fire me. We were both in agreement that it was clearly the Lord who spoke to my heart that morning, and it put both of us in a much easier position.

I was grateful of how that day panned out, even though I was again without a job. The one takeaway from this ordeal was that from that day on, I completely accepted the fact that I was a *stupid* guy and that my intelligence was undeniably below average. This job was a blessing in that it opened my eyes to this reality, and it was liberating as much as it was a little depressing. I do thank God for whatever kind of brain He gave me. May it one day bring Him glory.

6. RETURN TO SODOM AND GOMORRAH

*T*he job at the logistics firm was the start of a streak of unsuccessful job hunts for me. Prior to this job I had worked for a reputable company for over two years and resigned before they could fire me. I started out as a temp but got hired full on after a couple of months. I worked for the accounting department doing odd tasks for the people who had the *real* jobs. If this was Hollywood, it would be the equivalent of me working as a *waiter* at a fancy restaurant hoping to serve a big-time producer who would give me the big break. Instead, what happened was that I settled in to being *just* a waiter, got comfortable with the routine and became complacent. When I joined the company, it was during the middle of some major acquisition and things were a bit of a mess so they needed all the help they could get. But once things got settled and there was less need for the quality-of-life assistance that I provided, I didn't take the initiative to pursue more important responsibilities than pulling documents from the storage garage across the street. I was happy for the lighter workload and figured if they had something else for me, they'd let me know.

When people make excuses, they usually start by saying, *"I'm not making any excuses but,"* before proceeding with a laundry list of excuses as to why they failed. Well *I'm* not making any excuses, *but* there was a lot on my mind during this time. A good stretch of my employment with this company overlapped with my *troubled* relationship with Rochelle. There was constant turmoil in my life. During my stint with this company I had to endure the constant threat of breakups and the pain of actual breakups. I didn't have time to excel at my job or look at the *big picture*. Getting through the day was tough enough. So anyway, during one of our yearly evaluations, my boss hinted very strongly that I've reached a *dead end* with the company. After thinking about it for a couple of days, I decided to turn in my resignation with as much dignity as I could possibly muster. So I searched the newspapers and the internet to look for job openings. Having no college degree made it much harder to find *anything*. I did find a job doing whatever involving phones and stuff, which lasted about 5 weeks. The job was tedious and I had to drive way too far south of Orange County, so I quit. My cash reserves were running low. I had monthly car payments and rent to make. So I made the decision to move back in with my parents.

It wouldn't have been such a big deal if they didn't live in *Las Vegas*. That's right. When I moved out nearly two years earlier, my parents packed their bags and moved to Las Vegas, which was something they've been talking about for *years*. The main reason I moved out, as I had explained before, was so that I could have the space to deal with the breakup I was *anticipating* from Rochelle. However, the other reason was that my parents' questionable financial decisions made life *unstable*. I've lived through no less than *three* foreclosures with my parents. They insisted on buying homes they could not afford. In my early teens I didn't think much of it and just went with the flow. The older I got, the more I understood what was going on and the more *stress* I felt living with them. I admit being part of the problem as well, as I was pretty *materialistic* myself prior to becoming a Christian. After I got saved, however, I became the voice of reason and implored my parents to look for a smaller house that they could afford more easily. They didn't listen. So God opened doors for me and I took the opportunity to move out when it fell on my lap. But now it was time for me to move back in with my parents—in Vegas.

Some of my friends and roommates drove up to Vegas with me during the weekend I moved out. Then they had to drive back to Orange County, but I had to stay in Las Vegas with my parents. It was a sad, sad night for me. One of the first things I did was find a good church. In a place like Vegas, where all sorts of depravity are displayed on giant billboards, the first thing any believer needs to do is to get plugged into a church and have fellowship with other believers. I even managed to participate in some door-to-door preaching with a small group of new acquaintances.

So my job hunt in Vegas started. I found a temp job at a convention center, which was contracted for only a *week*. I needed the money so I took the job. A week's pay is a week's pay. I no longer had rent to worry about but I still needed to make payments for my car. Surprisingly, I found many job openings for which I was well qualified. I landed a lot of interviews within a short period of time. However, *none* of the companies wanted me. I got interview after interview but couldn't get myself hired. After two months living with my parents in Las Vegas, I moved out again and moved back into the previous place I was renting. When I had left, somebody *immediately* took my room. Coincidentally, when I could no longer stand Vegas and desperately wanted to move back to California, the guy who took my room *left*. Of course it was no coincidence. It was the Lord and His perfect *orchestration*. It took one phone call and I got my room back. I made the announcement to my parents that I was moving out and going back to my old place. I broke their hearts again, especially my dad's. As much friction as we had, my parents do love me in their own way and wanted me to live with them for as long as possible. But I *knew* that wasn't what the Lord wanted for me. No, it wasn't an audible voice or anything mystical, but the Lord has often guided me through *practical circumstances*. This time He led me back to the house I lived in before.

So I left my parents' house on a Friday evening, the day after Thanksgiving. My heart felt really, really *heavy* as I drove away. About an hour into my drive I took the next exit. I decided to drive back to my parents. About a half hour into my drive back, I took another exit, turned around and started heading back towards California again. After about another twenty minutes, I decided for good that I was going to turn back around and stay at my parents' for the night and drive to California in the morning. I did exactly that. I'm just thankful that I didn't turn into a *pillar of salt*. When I arrived at my parents' house I told them that I had a headache and didn't want to continue the drive that night. They were glad to see me back and when I left in the morning, my heart felt a lot lighter and so did theirs, I believe. It was a much more cordial goodbye with lots of positive vibes, like it was no big deal. After I moved back into my old place, it didn't take me long to find a good enough job that would sustain me for a little while. I knew then that I was exactly where the Lord wanted me to be.

7. ANOTHER THREE HOURS

*O*ne good thing that happened to me during the two months I spent in Las Vegas, was that I started talking to this girl over the *internet*. Her name was Tracy and she lived in Santa Maria, CA. She was sweet, smart, kind and looked like a much prettier version of *Chelsea Clinton*. She was also a Christian, or at least professed to be. If I got a nickel for every person I met who claimed to be Christian but with theology that might not necessarily support their claim, then I'd still be a very poor guy because I don't meet a lot of people. But if I were like most people and met as many people as normal people do, then I'd probably be financially secure if I got a penny for every professing Christian I met with *questionable* theology. At any rate, when I started talking to Tracy, she was sort of in the middle of not quite a relationship, but there was some man who has sort of been leading her on for a while but never really committing. Tracy and I became good friends in short order. I didn't beat around the bush, either, and expressed my interest in her. She *reciprocated*. We weren't exactly spring chickens. I was in my late twenties and she was only a couple of years younger. We didn't have time to play games. It was a breath of *fresh air*. The previous romantic interests I've had involved females who were a lot more immature and couldn't think for themselves. Tracy was different. She was very straightforward and honest. And she honestly was into *me*.

We continued to talk on the phone regularly after I moved back to Orange County. After a few weeks, the thing with the other guy just fizzled out, and our friendship grew into something much more. In fact, this was the most *intense* romantic experience I've had since *Rochelle*. I didn't think it was possible to ever feel that way again. I wish I could've recorded every phone conversation and every moment we spent together. You'd think it was fake because it was so perfect, like a script from a romantic movie. I was really into Tracy. She was the complete package. She was beautiful and she loved the Lord. What more can a Christian guy ask for?

We finally agreed to meet in person. I drove up to Santa Maria on a weekend in January. She was everything I had hoped she would be. There was no awkward transition from talking over the internet to standing in front of each other face to face. In the evening, we parked on a hilltop overlooking the ocean. It was a scene straight out of a (PG) movie. You could see the waves crashing against a cliff. We kissed in the car *passionately*. In an instant, whatever feelings I had left for Rochelle, were completely *erased*. Everything that has happened in my life has been leading to this moment, I thought, and the road I had to take to get here was irrelevant now. Sometimes though, I wish the Holy Spirit was a little less *subtle*. Earlier that day, Tracy took me to an uptown shopping district and bought me a hoodie. Then we went on a walk to a nearby beach town, filled with some of the nicest looking houses I've seen in my life. I commented, *"It's sad that most people who live in these houses probably don't know the Lord and will end up in hell."* What Tracy responded with was probably the last thing I expected to come out of her mouth. *"It doesn't mean that they can't have fun and enjoy this life,"* she retorted. I didn't know what to make of it. I was genuinely shocked. How could someone who claimed to be a follower of Jesus not care about the eternal destination of the lost? What was even more shocking was how I let her statement slide. I didn't even have anything to say about it. I liked Tracy too much and wasn't about to let a *silly* comment like that ruin the *romance*. Did you know that the Bible warns us that Satan can disguise himself as an angel of light?

Anyway, Tracy and I would see each other every weekend for the next three weeks. The following weekend she drove down to Orange County and we spent the entire day at *Disneyland*. The weekend after that I drove up to Santa Maria to watch the Super Bowl with her at one of her friend's house. To me that was significant as she didn't mind showing me off to her close friends. This was getting serious, I *hoped*. But as quickly as our relationship ascended, it went on a downward spiral over the next few days. Tracy started to behave weirdly. She was having some inner *turmoil*. You could say that she was *conflicted* over our relationship. Her ideal romance would involve basically a *rich* guy. You see, the more I talked to her, the clearer it became that she believed in what genuine Christians refer to as the *prosperity gospel.* In a nutshell, the prosperity gospel teaches that following Jesus would reap blessings of the financial and material kind. I was a poor guy, and Tracy had strong feelings for me. But she wouldn't commit.

The following Friday, I was at home and I saw Tracy appear online, so I sent her an instant message. She did not respond, which was unusual. I sent her another one a few minutes later, still no response. So I decided to give her a call to see what was going on. It kept on ringing, *no answer.* I began to freak out. I freak out easily over stuff like this. I never said I was perfect. I am "clingy" or "needy," after all. It turns out that Tracy just had to do some stuff in the kitchen and had to step out of the house for whatever reason. She was "*AFK.*" I found out because she told me that night; *in person.* That whole week had been emotionally draining for me due to the sudden and unexpected drama that came from Tracy. That Friday evening, I decided that I wasn't going to put up with it any longer. When Tracy did not pick up her phone, I immediately left my house and drove *three hours* to Santa Maria to find out what was going on. So I got there, and she was surprised to see me, naturally. Even I would tell you that it's not normal for people to drive three hours to someone's house unannounced. I didn't stay there long, I was just glad to see her. I probably did creep her the heck out, though, and her whole family as well. They probably thought I was psycho, and I don't blame them. It was a calculated risk, driving up to see her that night. I was determined to end the drama one way or *another.* If Tracy was *the one* the Lord had for me, then it wouldn't have mattered what I did. And if what I did would be enough to dissuade her from seeing me again, then she *clearly* wasn't the one, and I could live with that. It would be better than the perpetual drama I had with Rochelle, and I wasn't ever going to go through that *again.*

Had I kept my cool that evening and just waited for her to respond to my instant message, there was a good chance that Tracy and I would've gotten together for a long time, but I have no doubt that the end would've been the same, except it would've been much worse for me. Tracy was nice and sweet to me as always when I saw her that night. She even packed me a few slices of orange for my drive home. It was the last time I ever saw her, though we may have chatted a few times over the internet afterwards. She was in my life for less than three months, and it took three hours to end it for good.

8. DRUG ADDICT CONMAN UNCLE

*C*hristians are a work in progress; every single one of us. How do you know? Well, if you're still alive, then you're a work in progress. Until we receive our new bodies at the *rapture*, our spirit will always be at war with our flesh and we will struggle with sin. My absolute favorite hobby is playing video games. No, I'm not suggesting that's sinful. I mean, it *can* be. Anything can be sinful, depending on your heart's intent. Even going to church could be sinful if your motives are anything besides worshipping the Lord or learning more about Him. Anyway, I *love* video games. My generation grew up with video games and video games grew up with us. Everything great about video games today is the direct result of my generation's vision from when we were little kids imagining how awesome video games would be when we grew up. Everything stupid about video games today is the direct result of the younger generation of spoiled gamers who came around when most video games already looked good, but that's not what I wanted to talk about.

I love video games and I've bought just about every major console since the PlayStation 2. It's always exciting when there's a new console. The term *"next gen"* first became a thing during the PS2 era. Every gamer is eager to see the graphical capabilities of the latest console. For my generation, it's *always* been about the *graphics*. We didn't care about HD, 1080p or 4K, because any real gamer knows that resolution is *not* the same thing as *graphics*. I really don't understand the obsession with 4K and beyond these days. I get it, it's always better to have the best picture quality. But today's game developers are obsessed with pushing the highest resolution over actual graphics. I'm not fooled. Just think about this for a second. Jurassic Park came out over a *quarter of a century* ago. Yet today, no video game comes close to having the ultra-realistic graphics of the 480p dinosaurs from Jurassic Park.

After the PS2/Xbox era, the "next gen" was the Xbox 360, which made all sorts of impossible promises. It didn't matter to me. All I knew was that regardless of any exaggerated claims Microsoft may have made, it's still going to be *the* best console ever at the time. So I made a reservation at a local video game store to guarantee I would have one on the first day it came out. I reserved it several months before release. Somewhere along the line, for reasons I don't remember, I *cancelled* my reservation. Whatever the reason, all I know is that it was stupid. Now it just so happened that less than two weeks before launch, one of my friends bragged about not just having a reservation for an Xbox 360, but that his store guaranteed him *first shipment*. Apparently, getting one reserved didn't necessarily mean you would be able to get one at launch, as supplies were limited. So I *panicked*. The very next day, on my lunch break, I called the video game store just to "check" on my reservation. As I expected, they told me that my reservation was cancelled. I was prepared to play stupid and make a fuss about it, but something happened that I knew could only have been a small miracle from God. The guy on the phone told me that while the reservation money has been taken out of their system, my reservation remained. By God's grace, whoever did the transaction to cancel my reservation didn't do it quite right. So I told the guy that it was all a big mistake and that I was on my way to make full payment on the console. So I drove there and did exactly that. The attendant said to me that I was on the very *top* of the reservation list. When I told him that it was all a big mistake I was being honest. The mistake was that I *cancelled* my reservation, but that's not what I told him. I went on the offensive and asked the attendant what had happened to the money I put down, and from what he could tell in their computer, someone came in to withdraw the money, which is exactly what happened, that "somebody" being *me*. I did my best to look upset. I told him that I had an uncle who has the same full name as me, and that he was a drug addict, and he most likely came into the store, showed his I.D. and took out the money to pay for his *drug habit*. I pulled that out of thin air, and it scared me how good a liar I could be. The attendant believed me, accepted my full payment and *guaranteed* that I would have an Xbox 360 on day *one*.

I was quite proud of what I had achieved, but deep down I knew that I probably shouldn't have lied. I should've just trusted the Lord even with this petty thing that He knew I cared a lot about, especially after I found out that my reservation still stood despite the fact that the money was taken out. Instead, I resorted to *deception* to seal the deal. God chastised me. When I picked up my Xbox 360, mere moments after I drove out of the parking lot, my car battery died in the middle of a major street. I lived less than 10 minutes away but it took me *over two hours* to get home that night. I had to find somebody to help me push the car out of the way and into another parking lot, where I couldn't find anyone to give me a jump. I had to make several calls to get a hold of a friend, who finally came about an hour and a half later to give me a jump. That night was a big pain and I truly deserved it. I feel that I got off *easy*. God basically gave me a slap on the wrist, but I sure learned my lesson that night. It wasn't a new lesson for me, but apparently one that I needed to be reminded of.

9. WHO'S (REALLY) THE BOSS

I believe that a Christian's life is filled with many *"God moments"*—situations in which God's involvement is so *undeniable*. I've had plenty of them to be sure, but I think there have been *countless* others that weren't so obvious to me. I guess if I want to be technical, *every* single moment is a "God moment," as the Lord is in every single facet of our life, being, and existence. Depending on your walk with God, that should either comfort or terrify you. We know that God is *omnipresent*. It's a difficult concept to grasp. In fact, it's literally impossible to understand with our *fallen* brains. A lot of things that the Bible reveals to us won't fully make sense until we get to the other side of eternity. I believe God designed it this way to make room for *faith*. If we were to fully scrutinize and weigh every ounce of evidence that proves the Bible as God's very word, we would be amazed that it even takes faith to believe it.

But we are sinners and are all guilty of *unbelief* to varying degrees. God's word ought to be enough, and it truly is. But oftentimes, the Lord will do certain things to remind His children that He is with us even when our circumstances might suggest otherwise. I'm sure we've all been in desperate situations that made us cry out to the Lord, only to get nothing but apparent *silence* in return. It can be beyond frustrating at times. I confess that even the pettiest matters could get me to question God's love for me. I mean, it's so easy for the Lord to instantly right every wrong and fill every lack in my life, but somehow He refuses to. But God's not the granter of wishes. He's no *genie*. He doesn't bow down to my will; I bow down to His.

I've asked the Lord a ton of things throughout my life, and some of them have been downright *absurd*. But there are some things that I won't even bother praying about because to me they are way past ridiculous. One such thing was a worsening situation I was in the middle of at one of my previous jobs. I was hired as a project coordinator at an industrial air conditioning company, and I'm pretty sure my boss *regretted* hiring me. I wasn't bad at my job at all, but our personalities weren't compatible. We didn't clash or anything, but the way I conducted myself just generally rubbed him the wrong way. I have good reason to believe that it was *spiritual warfare*. My boss began to show less and less patience towards me, even though my performance didn't demand his patience. He was quick to blame me for any issue that arose, never looking into the facts first before passing on judgment. His priority was to get his *yell on*. Yet if it turned out, as it often did, that whatever it was had *nothing* to do with my actions, he wouldn't so much as apologize to me. It got to the point where he was just always short with me no matter what. There were no good days anymore. It was a little intimidating.

One day, I didn't do something quite the way he would've done it. I don't remember exactly what it was, but I did absolutely nothing wrong; just differently from how he would've handled the matter. He yelled at me in the middle of the office and basically had an outburst. It would've made for a comical if not cliché scenario for a movie, where the boss is portrayed as a humorless hothead who constantly screamed at their subordinates. However in real life, it was very unprofessional and turned the working environment *hostile* for me. It was *degrading*. I hung my head low for the rest of that day, which was a Friday. It affected me throughout the weekend and even made me feel a bit *depressed*. I called my supervisor on Monday morning and told her that I wouldn't be able to make it to work that day. I couldn't bear the thought of having to deal with my boss's hostility. I felt helpless. It may have been different if I could speak my mind without consequence. I didn't feel any better on Tuesday morning and I once again called in sick.

I couldn't hide forever so I finally showed up to work on Wednesday. Later that morning my department was called in to my boss's office for an *impromptu* meeting. It was the last thing I wanted to do. At least my co-workers were with me, which I hoped would push my boss to act more civil towards me. To say that I was apprehensive would be a major understatement. After we all got situated, I noticed that everyone was there *except* for my boss. Another boss dude from a different department was conducting the meeting. One of the first things that he mentioned was that my boss *no longer worked for the company.* He didn't elaborate, but the details hardly mattered to me. All I knew was that I missed work because of him, and when I returned, he was gone for good. I couldn't believe my ears. A massive feeling of relief came over me, immediately followed by thankfulness, then humility, then joy. *God literally fired my boss.* I didn't even have to pray about it. I didn't even think of praying about it because to me, it was just one of those silly things that God would never even consider. To me, asking God to fire someone is not much different from asking Him to strike someone down with some horrible disease. It's not a thing I could ask the Lord with a clear conscience. But He knew what I've been going through. God *delivered* me from an ugly situation. It was a reminder that I could trust Him in any circumstance and that He's got my back even when it didn't feel like it. It also served as a reminder for future incidents that would be just as *oppressive.* God knows what's going on behind the scenes. When certain people seem like they're out to get me and the Lord's not doing a thing about it, perhaps it's because those people really aren't out to get me and God doesn't need to intervene. It's been said that when the Lord puts you through the furnace, He keeps His hand on the thermostat. Not a quote from the Bible, obviously, but nonetheless in line with Scripture if you take into account God's character as it's been revealed within the pages of the Bible.

10. THE SOLO GIG

*O*ne of my biggest disappointments in life is that I was never able to make a living out of playing my sax. As I've mentioned before, I wasn't looking for fame or fortune. A *little* fortune maybe. *Supplementary* income even. Getting paid for doing something you would gladly do for free is everybody's dream. To me though, it was more than just the money. It was about having a gift that not everyone had. It was about having something of *value*, something uniquely mine that people would find worth paying for to experience. But it was not meant to be. I suppose it *could* still happen, but highly unlikely. I have musical talent, but I'm not the most talented musician in the world. I do have enough talent to bless *some* people. I am grateful for my lot. I enjoy performing for people. Admittedly part of that is my *flesh*. I wish I could say otherwise, but I do get some satisfaction from being able to show off my stuff. The other part of it is *love*. It's not just words when I say that I want to bless people with my music. Music can inspire and lift up the spirit. A familiar tune could rekindle one's favorite memories. When some people hear an instrumental version of a song they love, the moment they recognize the tune usually brings instant *delight*. It's these types of blessings that I want to give others through my music. It's just hard to find opportunities to do so. For one thing, I didn't have a band. That's mostly it.

One time, though, I was determined to *perform*. I had the energy and excitement. I felt *inspired*. I was introduced to a guitarist by one of the vocalists from the worship team I played with. He was a versatile player and could play a variety of styles. He had a lot of professional experience and though my style of music wasn't exactly his cup of tea, he was cool enough to agree to accompany my sax with his guitar. I wanted to play at an outdoor shopping mall in Orange County. I've watched plenty of musicians do it. *"Busking"* is a common term for it.

For this particular venue, though, I first needed to get permission from the management in order to secure a spot and a time slot. So I sent them a video of me and my guitarist buddy doing a cover of Eric Clapton's *"Tears in Heaven."* The management approved. It was a cold December night in Southern California and we set up near the sidewalk where there was plenty of foot traffic. It was my ideal playing atmosphere. I wasn't the *center* of attention but I provided good music for passersby and onlookers. Most people were indifferent and didn't care one way or another about my music, but there were a few who stopped to watch for a while. In case you were wondering, we did set up a container for people to throw money into if they chose. That's all part of "busking." It wasn't a paid gig. Like I mentioned, it's something I'd gladly do for free, and I was doing it that night.

It was the first time I had acted as my own *agent* to pursue a gig, and it was overall a success. I played a selection of contemporary songs and threw in a couple of my own. We played two sets that lasted a little an under an hour each. It was a great experience for me as it was the only time I've done a "concert" of my own, where I was in charge of the entire playlist and acted as the musical director. Yes, I realize I played with only one other musician, but I called the shots nonetheless, and my vision for that evening panned out pretty much the way I had expected. It was very laid back and I was loose, playing to the best of my ability with hardly any pressure on myself besides seeing the whole thing through all the way to the end. It was a major *accomplishment* for me. I made this thing happen, marketed myself and got the show on the *road*, almost literally. I had my moments that evening, the most I ever had. For me, it was a night to remember. And by the end of it all, when we counted all the money, we had accumulated a *whopping* $17. The guitarist was gracious enough to let me have all of it. I mean, it was serious chump change and this guy's been around. He basically did charity by agreeing to back me up that night, and I'm perfectly fine with that.

11. THE HONEST LIAR

First off, I'd like to thank you for making it all the way to the end of this book. That is, of course, if you didn't merely skip ahead and stuff. I'd like to close it with a question, more like a riddle and a conundrum, which I'm proud to have come up with on my own. Now I'm *not* at all making claims that it's an *original* thought. I wouldn't be surprised if someone else had already come up with it hundreds of years ago. Regardless, it's something that I thought of myself. I didn't get it from anyone else, whether or not someone had already posed the very same question I'm about to present. I'm quite proud of it. You know me, *little man, little brain*, I feel quite *brilliant* for this. It's something I always keep in my pocket, ever ready to whip it out whenever an opportunity arises. It rarely ever does, though, so I'm making my own opportunity here. Without further ado, I present to you, *"The Honest Liar."* This is the question: *If a man who lies 100% of the time admits that he lies 100% of the time, is he lying for telling the truth?* Think about that for a minute and let it sink in. Pretty good, eh? Yup, I came up with that! Or maybe it's just plain nonsense that's so un-brilliant, even a chimp could've come up with it. Oh well.

AFTERWARDS

I don't know what to call this entry. At the very start of this book, I wrote a "preface" and called it that. I was going to use "foreword," but I learned that a foreword is written by someone else besides the author. I thought of calling it a "prologue" but found out that the term mainly applies to novels and stuff. I'm pretty confident that "preface" was the right thing to call the introduction section of this book (and yes, I thought of calling it "Introduction," but there were some technical issues on that as well). However, I couldn't figure out what to call *this* section. It's the opposite of preface, but I couldn't really find anything on the internet on what the proper term is. I know that "prologue" doesn't apply, so that ruled out "epilogue." So I did some more Googling and even ran upstairs to look through some of the autobiographies on my bookshelf to see what they called the ending part of the book, and I still couldn't find anything conclusive. So alas, I landed with *"afterwards."* I think it's fitting. It's sort of inspired by "foreword," and since "afterword" is like its actual opposite, I couldn't use that, either. So here we are, at last, at the *Afterwards.*

When I started writing this book, I didn't intend for it to be necessarily chronological. I mean, generally speaking, I wanted it to have some sort of order, divided into four sections of my years, beginning with my elementary school age and so forth. I decided that anything I wrote within each section didn't have to be chronological. However, the more recent the memory, the easier it was to know which events took place first, so as I got to the later parts of this book, the stories were written down pretty much in the actual order they happened, for the most part, though I'm still not 100% sure. At the time of this writing, the last entry on this book (not counting "The Honest Liar), "The Solo Gig," took place about eleven and a half years prior. Needless to say, a lot of things have transpired since then. Mostly wonderful things. In fact, overwhelmingly wonderful things. Life's not gone on without a hitch, but I have very little to complain about if I'm being honest. Could things be better? Of course. Could it be worse? Absolutely. My life's not been filled with spectacle, and in most cases, I believe that's a good thing. I think being on the sidelines is underrated. We all want our share of the spotlight, but in life, I think being simply a spectator could be as rewarding as you make it out to be.

Right now I'm amused with the current events. Most of this book was written during the COVID-19 stay-at-home quarantine of 2020. I'm blessed to be one of the few who get to work full-time from home throughout this ordeal. But in my line of work, during this whole crisis, it pains me to see how stupid and selfish people are. Most companies aren't thinking straight. They are making irrational decisions, hoarding as much as they can and diminishing everybody else's supplies. It's *foolish*. Is their goal to survive or simply be *the last man standing*? If companies want to not merely survive but to *thrive*, don't they realize they need other companies to do business with? It's all connected. You can have it all to yourself and be the last man standing, but you will fall, inevitably, just like everybody else, if there's nobody else around to provide the goods and services that you need to survive. Companies don't seem to understand that. They simply want the lion's share of everything so that they can starve to death after everybody else has.

The great thing is that the Lord is still in control. I don't know if life will ever go back to normal. A lot of damage has been done to the world's economies and I'm not sure if all of it can be repaired, and if so to what extent. But Jesus is the same yesterday, today and forever. We can all take shelter in that truth. There are very powerful men out there today who are convinced they are the ones pulling all the strings, but one day they will have to answer for their actions. God is not mocked, nor does He ever slumber. I for one cannot wait for the *Day of the Lord*. This is the final thought I'd like to leave you: The Day of the Lord. Look it up and find out what it truly entails because it's not really the kind of day most people think it is when they sing, *"This is the day that the Lord has made."* Peace out.